MW01480715

Lucy Smiles About . . .

Anna~
I hope this book
makes you smile before
having sweet dreams and
perhaps reminds you that
we all have it inside of us
to live the life our dreams,
too!

Love
Lucy Smiles
xoxo

Lucy Smiles About . . .

Lucy Smiles

Copyright © 2009 by Lucy Smiles.

Library of Congress Control Number: 2009901750
ISBN: Hardcover   978-1-4415-1494-3
               Softcover   978-1-4415-1493-6

All rights reserved. No part of this book may be reproduced or transmitted in
any form or by any means, electronic or mechanical, including photocopying,
recording, or by any information storage and retrieval system, without permission
in writing from the copyright owner.

This book was printed in the United States of America.

To order additional copies of this book, contact:
Xlibris Corporation
1-888-795-4274
www.Xlibris.com
Orders@Xlibris.com
59600

Contents

Introduction ix

Dedication xiii

Acknowledgements xv

A Very Special Thank You xix

Don't Mind If I Do 3

Wide Open Spaces 5

Of Course! 7

Truly, Madly, Deeply 9

Void If Removed 11

Caller ID 13

Reason Being 15

Trivial Pursuit 17

Just One of Those Things 19

Road Work Ahead 21

Put a Sock in It 23

Are We There Yet? 25

I Beg to Differ! 27

Well, since you Put it That Way! 29

Cut to the Chase 31

Peace Out! 33

Bugger Off! 35

Yours, Truly 37

Truth Be Told 39

If the Shoe Fits 41

Works for Me! 43

Just Like That! 45

Under the Circumstances 47

Above All Else 49

Beside Myself! 51

Top of the Morning to You! 53

Not So Fast! 55

Wait a Minute 57

"Wishful Thinking" 59

I Believe So 61

How Are You? 63

Point Taken 65

Static Cling 67

One Moment, Please 69

Mighty Oaks from Little Acorns Grow 71

What's My Line? 73

You Are Cordially Invited 75

Sticky Notes 77

Please Do! 79

Cruise Control 81

By The Way 83

Slippery When Wet 85

Dream On! 87

Off The Rack 89

Motion Picture 91

The Tie That Binds 93

We'll See 95

So Far, So Good! 97

Alarm Will Sound 99

Handle with Care 101

Who Am I Kidding? 103

It Goes Without Saying 105

One Fell Swoop 107

Fuel to the Fire 109

If You Will 111

Check, Please! 113

Raise the Bar 115

Front and Center..117
Let Sleeping Dogs Lie 119
Musical Chairs 121
Once Upon A Time 123
Members Only 125
Inquire Within 127
Enough Already 129
Make Your Mark 131
Baggage Claim 133
By The Book..135
Out on a Limb 137
Please Stand Clear..139
None the Less 141
BYOB..143
Enter at Your Own Risk 145
Divide and Conquer..147
Phone a Friend 149
Surround Sound 151
No Purchase Necessary..153
Hold on for Dear Life 155
Come Again? 157
However 159
"Light as a Feather" 161
Strong as an Ox 163
Statue of Liberty 165
Under the Influence 167
Opening Statement 169
Right Turn Only..171
How Thoughtful! 173
I'll be the Judge of That 175
Bona Fide..177
Shuck It..179
Oh My!..181
Carry On Now..183

And Action! 185

Press Release 187

It's Beyond Me! 189

Spare Me 191

Get Out! 193

La Vie En Rose 195

Cornerstone 197

Love, Actually 199

Don't Mind If I Don't 201

In Closing 203

Introduction

Lie still. Keep your heels together and your hands by your side with your palms up. Don't think of anything but being here, now. Breathe normally through your nose, and just be. Lie still.

> "I wonder if that eye shadow will go with my new skirt."
> "Cute guy—I am sure he has a girlfriend."
> "If I eat a whole celery stalk before my meal, does my meal lose calories? How does that work exactly? Maybe I won't even be hungry for my meal after that!"

How many of us, either through group meditation, yoga or any other form of relaxation method have actually been able to tune out completely?

I have participated in many sessions, many different forms of getting into my soul, the deepest parts of my inner self, and really tried to pay attention to "now" and "being with."

I have to be honest. I am able and accepting of paying attention to my breathing, since I realize many of the times I am not breathing at all. I am also very much paying attention to more than I normally would because now I have been asked not to.

I am not here to claim to be an inspirational guru, a spiritual leader or a motivational master.

I have not studied for years in India nor have I ever spoken in front of an audience to educate my insight to the world. I have never even been overseas and I only just finally took the initiative to get my passport, two years ago just after turning 30.

So why are you reading what I am writing?

Well, I am hoping it is because you relate to what I have to say, simply because we have all at one point or another, felt similar emotions, have been through the similar experiences, if even generally speaking, and we all have the biggest thing in common—we think.

The writings of this book came to be because there are so many thoughts in my head that I needed to get them out.

What better way to get them out of my head than to get them into yours?

So, though I haven't mastered the world of e-commerce, I haven't created a fool proof system for financial freedom, and I certainly haven't found the seven secret steps to a successful life-long relationship with our partners, I have put a lot of thought into this.

We have so much to say and spend so much time saying it to ourselves, that we neglect the true communication with all those around us.

My intention for this book is to help you, if perhaps even just to shift your thoughts for a moment. Since the majority of our thoughts are negative, I claim this book to be of purpose. In fact, I am positive!

I am not going to research neurological findings or pharmaceutical and alternative methods of medication to perhaps enhance or completely alter our thoughts, either.

I will leave that to the professionals!

I am here to have fun, make you laugh or even make you cry, if you wish, or need to. Maybe my "smiles" will be just like the stories in your mind. You will be that much more relieved that at least one other person on this earth has experienced the same thing or similar; or at least one other person on this earth is willing to admit it! There is no workbook attached, but perhaps this will help you work on admitting certain things about your life and allow you to perhaps take action where you were otherwise afraid to.

Lastly, this book may allow you to take hold of what is near and dear to your heart or bring those in your life closer to your heart.

Whatever the case, I am hopeful that after reading this book of smiles, you can take with you many lessons, many new and bright ideas, of what it means to live with a purpose and what it means to accept yourself, through good and bad, pretty and ugly, bitter or ever so sweet.

If perhaps, after reading this book, it leaves a bad taste in your mouth, then I apologize. I cannot get those hours back for you. But I will thank you now for giving me those hours, as help in supporting my passion to write a book that will be read by at least one other person beside my editor.

(Oh, I love even just saying that I have an editor!)

Not to mention, as the universe claims ever so generously, you get back tenfold of what you give, so if anything you actually did yourself a favor by supporting me in this scary journey to share my smiles.

Please, don't close the book just yet.
Remember what I said about tenfold?
Thank you!

Love Lucy Smiles

Dedication

This book is dedicated to my Lucy Smiles,
my big sister and biggest supporter
in my life, Yvonne.
Without your hand to hold mine
and your heart to love me unconditionally,
none of my book would exist.

There is not one part of my childhood growing up,
where you were not right by my side, making sure that I was cared for,
loved and safe.

Since I could remember, we have been called the 2 Lucys,
and always will be attached at the hip,
no matter how far our lives take us on our journey.

Lucy Smiles

It always seems, no matter what is going on in your life,
you always have to make sure I am ok. Any time I feel I am falling,
you are there to pick me up. Every time I am afraid to move forward,
you remind me why I must keep going.

How did I get so blessed to have a big sister and best friend like you?
Some questions are better left unanswered.

If I can only be there for you as much as you are for me,
it is all I will do to be sure you know how special you are.

I love you Lucy. Every word in this book has been written,
thanks to your presence in my life.

Love,
Little Lucy

Acknowledgements

I would like to acknowledge the enormous support and friendships of so many of you who have changed my life, and shifted my thoughts, which allowed me to write.

For my Goddesses, you all know who you are; but a special thanks to: Aunt Sue, thank you. You always know. Cindy, Cassandra, and Christina—Our stumbles into each others' lives will always take my breath away! As we say "You can't make this stuff up!"

Jenn Simpson—"Something has got to be done, so we are just going to have to do something" Our mantra from the college years! No matter how far we are, we always know that the day will indeed come, that we are sitting on our porch together, with our hot milky tea, and our green slacks, and perms. Goddess, help us!

Christine Seguin—From creating playhouses in your basement to creative fantasy business plans for 3 Girls. Inc, there has never been a dull moment for us. From 13 to 31, we have stuck through together through bad boyfriends and bad hair days.
Thanks for always making me laugh!

Phebes—Let's be honest! The word "Magic" in my life has your name all over it! You are my favorite travel partner and SUC Rock Star! Anything I can do to support you, like you have supported me, just say the word!

Susan—You are why I believe in my Goddess strengths, as a woman, as a warrior.

Vanessa—We obviously still have some magical work to do together, so our reconnection at 6am one summer morning came early, and I plan on many more memories ahead! I could go on. Goddesses from A (Anne, Amanda) to Z (Zahra), but that would be a whole other book.

I must attempt to balance out all of that beautiful feminine energy with some masculine energy, if that is at all possible.

I will start with my Guardian Angel, Roger.
We have had ups and downs, enough to learn as much about ourselves through each other in as little time as humanly possible. We grow most from those we are most resistant to, as they carry the deepest mirrors to our souls that sometimes we wish to not see.
Thank you for taking my hand, and on more occasions than I wished for, making me face my mirror to remind me of how beautiful, powerful and amazing I can be, when I felt otherwise. You have always been with me. And you know in your heart, that your pushes, mostly while I kicked and screamed, are what made most of this book transform from thoughts to words. You will always be my best friend, no matter where our paths lead.

Jacques.
You took me in at the most pivotal times in my career successes, and allowed me to shine without worry. Your generous hospitality has enormously impacted my growth.

Ray.
You turned the nasty Vancouver rain into sunshine when I never thought the clouds had a possibility of separating. Whether through love, support, or care, you held out your hand with no expectation from me, and helped me to grow as the independent woman I always hoped to be.

To my many other amazing and magical connections, I am so blessed for your belief in who I am and what I stand for and still strive to stand for.

My Parents—Without you, I would not be here. Thank you for always being here for me. My childhood was nothing short of wonderful. My memories are that of laughter, smiling and sunshine, thanks to your guidance and belief in my path.

And last but certainly never least, my editor, Michael Meade. People come into our lives, not realizing how much of an impact they will have. Though you always remain behind the scenes in my life, your energy and presence is at the forefront of my mind for this book. I am blessed that someone of your stature, credibility, but more importantly your immeasurable talent would take the time to help a little girl, like me, on her way.

A Very Special Thank You

Julius. The wisest, cutest, and cuddliest puppy in the world, or so says me. I've had the pleasure of having your unconditional love by my side throughout the most drastic changes in my life.

From moving across the country, to moving our way over the bridges of Vancouver's many troubled waters, and beautiful sunrises. It was our walks together, and your companionship that gave me the confidence to be who I want to be. Perhaps I was envious of your carefree attitude of only knowing what was here, and what was now, and living it out as such.

But every time I looked in your eyes, I could hear your voice telling me that I could give it just a little bit more.

You are my sweetest Soul Mate.
My creative journey started with our magical morning journey together, and so my first smile has your precious face written all over it.

Love,
Mom

Many people say
"I wouldn't chance it!"
I say
"Chances are I will."

LoVe,
LuCy sMiLeS

"If you want to see unconditional love, look at
life through the eyes of animals and children
and you needn't search any further."

Don't Mind If I Do

How many relationships, connections and even quick interactions have we experienced that have given us messages we could take personally into our own lives to help us see things in a different light?

When others share their stories, their dreams, and even their "opinionated" thoughts on things that they have been through, there is always a part of us that takes part of their story to use for our own good.

We are all here to share our thoughts and experiences to help others to perhaps see circumstances more objectively and ponder things in ways they may not have really tuned in to.

Just as our friends don't mind telling us their opinions on things, we must be able to listen, sit with, and decide if their opinion does actually strike in us something that we can use, or something we can thank them for, and from this, what we need to understand—from within.

Hindsight is 20/20, and we have a 50/50 chance of either using or tossing our friends' advice.
Either way, we must hold our friends dear and very close to our hearts since they do have our best interest at heart.

So, my best advice in the matters of the heart, are to listen, and look within . . .

And if, by chance, you chose to go with the gang, be sure you have your best interest at heart, as you are the best judge for what's best for you.

Thank You . . . Don't Mind if I Do!

"I figured out I can have anything my heart desires, as long as my heart is in the right place. Go figure."

Wide Open Spaces

Each of us has an energy field around us that whether or not we believe it, can pretty much carry us to the ends of the Earth.

It is a matter of our choice on how closed or how open we wish to be. To add to that, our vibrations also play a big role in our happiness and in how happy those around us are. We are all so influenced by our friends and loved ones, so much that many times we can take on their energy and vibrations, without recognizing it, hindering our personal growth.

Do you ever notice your behavior or your state of being can be quite different depending on the different people with whom you surround yourself?
People you automatically laugh with without even saying word.
People you hold your tongue or your thoughts from.

While it is our responsibility to be true to ourselves and not blame others for putting us in certain "moods" or negative mindsets, we do, as highly empathetic human beings, allow for this to take place.

We all have it in us to be the best we can be and we all learn from each other things about ourselves to help us on that path to greatness!

It is also important, however, while finding our true selves to stay true to ourselves and do all that we can to make the best choices for ourselves, whatever that may be to keep us at the best vibration.

This helps others rise high to the occasion and be successful.

So, take time out to help your friends and all those you love. But be sure that you are making the best choices for yourself, first, and you will be able to best help them.
It is never selfish to take care of yourself. It actually would be selfish not to.

"No matter the issue, if you chose love in all that you do, you are choosing life at its best for you."

Of Course!

No matter where we go, on our journey of life, it will always be the right place.
We carry ourselves almost to the ends of the earth, in search for our
personal purpose.

May times we may feel lost and confused,
not sure which path is the right for us.
Are we on course?

Of course!

And then, there comes a place we stand, where all our confusion
changes to confidence.

This is when you know you are home.
This is when you realize you are where you are to be.
This is always the case, but our thoughts are what allow us to either
feel lost or feel found.

We don't always get there right away.
Sometimes we are there for only so long; leave, and only to come back
full circle in appreciation
for being back.

If we wish to always be in the best place, we must also remember and
embrace that which makes our heart the warmest, and where it happens.
We must do all that we can to remain in that place.

Remember, on days when you feel like you cannot find you; you are
where you are meant to be, and that is just the right place, of course.

By being in the best frame of mind, you will find yourself in the
absolutely best place in time!

"If you can't give it your all then don't do it at all."

Truly, Madly, Deeply

If I had all the answers, chances are I would be typing in my own private Villa somewhere in the heart of Spain, sipping on a margarita and nibbling on tapas.

As it has it, looking around where I really am typing, it looks like I still have some research to do.

We all have the opportunity, just as fairly as the next person, to have all the world has to offer.

The key to getting to that place we drool over is to be sure that what we are doing is what we truly, madly and deeply love.

Spending warm nights with gentle breezes and luxuries beyond our wildest dreams may not happen overnight. But when we put our all into things, we will reap the benefits. It is just a matter of time and patience while doing it.

It's a world of wonder and a world of wonderful offerings. Believe in yourself enough that you can take in all the air and breathe from the deepest part of your heart.

Choose things to do that excite your heart and soul.

"What if any thoughts that are not allowing us to walk forth with great passion and drive, once removed, they are automatically VOID?"

Void If Removed

Don't you love those warranties on so many different material items we buy?
"Void if removed"
If we can take these ever so important warnings and use them to our
own benefit,
perhaps we have a whole new way of thinking?

Quite literally!

I had a very inspirational message come to me the other day on this very
subject from a dear beautiful friend of mine.

Simple suggestion . . .
Whatever concerns and conditions that are less than comforting,
acknowledge them, removed them, and leave them in the caring hands of the
Universe to handle.

Don't forget to say thanks!
Once you have done this, remind yourself that they are now officially
VOID and can no longer use up any of your mind space.

If you're anything like me, in doing this exercise you will now have a lot
of free space.
Imagine the freedom.

"When life calls on that which you don't understand, don't question. Just answer!"

Caller ID

How many times does your phone ring, you look at the number, and decide not to bother picking it up?

How many of those times is it because you know who it is, since the number is right there in front of you, and perhaps it just isn't someone you wish to speak to at the moment?

Other times, the number is unknown, and again,
we decide not to dignify it with a response, just in case.
Besides phone call identification, many other issues in our lives deal with callings, identifying them for what they are, and the decision as to whether or not we will respond at all.

Every one of us has a special calling while we are here on Earth. Many of us have not yet identified what this calling is, and that is simply fine, as we may not be ready to take on all that we are here to take on.
We are still preparing.

But once we do clearly see our calling, and have identified it as ours,
we must look beyond our fears,
our programs and our insecurities
and simply take the call.

"Stop trying to find all the reasons why you can't and start being more reasonable!"

Reason Being

If you could do anything you wanted, whenever you wanted,
wherever you wanted, what would that look like to you?
Does that mirror your life, right now?
I can bet a select few of us just stood back, perhaps with an uneasy
shrug of
"Are you kidding me?" Am I right?

May I be so bold as to ask "How many of your past few years replicate
the ones before that?"
If everything in life is impermanent, why do so many of our days mirror
each other, and so many of our thoughts mirror each other as well?

The vicious cycle here is that we cannot very well expect changes,
great changes, great exponential increases in our life's spiritual,
emotional and financial richness, if we don't take into account how it is
we are going to get there.

What we do need to improve upon is that we need to do something, as
opposed to nothing at all, expecting for the change to take place on its own.

Granted, some of us have the simple luck of striking it rich and having
our lives change drastically without us having to lift a finger.

But, let's be honest. Of all the people you know, how many of these
people are those people?

Now get up, stand up, and show up in your life.
You are the most important person in this relationship,
and if you act as though you are ok to play the field, and not commit,
you will only get that back.

So, it's up to you. I say this to you, reason being:
We all have a reason—being.
What's yours?

"In life, if I am the Teacher and the Student, can I still skip school?"

Trivial Pursuit

Many of us are in search for what lies beneath all the traditional ways of living, whether it is about making money, spiritual growth, or personal relationships.

We are actually in a day and age where we are exposed to so many new and exciting ways to attain success, on all levels.

Whether it is internet-based businesses, and deciding to self-employ online communities for growing relationships, or local groups and organizations to allow us to expand our horizons, we have our hands full of opportunities.

Like anything else, however, just as there are numerous ideas and opinions from a multitude of mediums to help guide us on our way, one thing must remain in place.
We are unique and individual and what works for one may not, in fact, work for another.
So, be assertive in your search for your authentic self and take pride in your own part you are playing in life.

We are all in pursuit of our passions.
Yet we must be sure we are following with a faithful focus that is true to our needs and not following suit to someone else's path.

Enjoy the ride, and share the road. Just be sure you are in the driver's seat.

"I think I can; I think I can; I know I can . . . I just
don't know where to begin . . ."

Just One of Those Things

Some days it's almost like we cannot remember that we had a weekend.
Saturday and Sunday are long gone and we are already into the
swing of things.

Waking up refreshed and ready is one thing, but trying to remember
what we have going on even yesterday can take a toll.

No matter what line of work we are in, we all have lists of things to do
and we all have a list of things we would much rather do.

Most of the time, the hardest part of the "To Do" list is to know where
to begin. Any time we tackle the tasks we always realize our efforts to
execute things are less energy draining than the worrying, wondering
and wasting of time not wanting to get started.

Just because we have a million things on our plates, doesn't mean we have
to do everything at once, or even think of more than one thing at a time.

My suggestion for time management is do one thing at a time, and take
your time doing it.

Stop wasting your time worrying about absolutely everything else
that you have to do that you are not doing, while you are trying to do
everything else.
Believe me, those things will be there waiting patiently for you to start them.

It's just one of those things . . .

"Not following my dreams must feel worse
than following them . . . I think I will follow them,
then decide."

Road Work Ahead

I know if you are like me, you are a creature of habit. As we very well know, we cannot continue to do the same things and expect different results. And that is fine if what we are doing is creating the most outstanding results on a daily basis from our work. There is no telling how much momentum is created by taking our passions or dreams one step further. I walk the same way, pretty much every day, for my hour walk-out of my house and around a large block to get to the coffee shop. Once out the door of the coffee shop, I continue to make a full clockwise journey back to my home. I make it full circle.

One morning I decided to take it one extra large block, just going further before making the same path back. While I was in the coffee shop I decided I may go back the same way I came instead of my usual way around.

As I left the coffee shop with my coffee, I automatically continued "forward" and realized I was not going to take the way "back" that I came. To my sweet surprise, I ran into an old dog, 16 years old, name Lucky. I stopped and stared into his eyes. The owner said no one ever stops to pet him as they are afraid.

As I said goodbye and walked way, I felt this sense of blessing for life and making the small things really count. I choked up thinking of the dog. I turned around to discover that the dog had followed me half a block.

I petted him again and thanked him for reminding me how lucky I am. As I walked forward, I came across a sign that read "Road Work Ahead." None of this would have happened if I had backtracked. I wouldn't have met "Lucky" and I wouldn't have realized that going the extra step pays off. Life does come full circle. You just have to believe in every step as creating your path to the next. But you must take action and work for what you want in life.

As luck would have it, no one can do it for you.
But it is worth it in the end.

"There is something to be said for silence."

Put a Sock in It

There isn't too much that floors me anymore.
I have seen it, done it, thought it, and wrote this book about it. I know a
thing or two about taking thoughtful consideration in choosing
my thoughts.

We have choices in life, but our choices are a projection of what we
believe and from our thoughts we create all that surrounds us.

If I had a penny for every nervous, negative, and worry some thought—
which usually has a lot to do with financial security—I would be
financially free! It's crazy.

Think about it.
At the end of the day, as much as we would thoroughly enjoy having it
all, we all simply want to be sure that we are cared for, financially, so we
can enjoy all that life has to offer without worry.

We have more in common than we realize.
But if our common thoughts are focusing on the scarcity in our lives
and wondering how we will get through when times are tough we don't
make way for building on solutions resulting in building the financial
dynasty that we all know we have in us.

We have our ups and downs and times will get tough, however, if we can
transform our thoughts to create a positive shift, we may knock our
socks off with the results!

Perhaps when you notice yourself getting carried away with negative
voices, you can start by
putting a sock in it.

"Not only do I wonder if I am almost there yet; but sometimes I am not even sure where I am going . . ."

Are We There Yet?

All of us have heard it. We have asked it.
"How much longer until we reach the final destination so we can start living?"

All of us are here working on ourselves and working whether for ourselves, or someone else, so we can finally get to that place! You know that place?

That place where once we reach it will make this all worthwhile. The headaches, the long days, the sweat, you name it, it will be worth it. The place where it will all make sense, where we can finally sit back, kick our feet up and say "The ride was long, bumpy, and a bit exhausting, but we made it."

We have visions of what it will look like.
The water is crystal blue, the air is clear and the sun always shines. It's so exciting we can almost smell it.

But then we come back to reality and realize we still have a ways to go. We are hoping we took the right turn that is going to get us there, untouched and unharmed, and not to mention, soon. We are still healing from the few bruises and scars we endured when the vehicle broke down and we had to walk part of the way on foot, falling over our feet a few times.

But it will be worth it once we get there.

There is no right or wrong on the road we are on. The only thing to know is we are where we are right now and that will always be the right place to get to
where we are going. And, if you are wondering if you are almost there yet, the answer is, "Yes, you are."

"If your life were up for grabs,
how quick would you grab hold of it?"

I Beg to Differ!

I remember elementary school, high school and college.
I am surprised I survived all three.

But I am here now and there is something to be said for that. When we are growing—in height, in age, in our skin—we are also responsible for growing and learning as much as we need to in school, and also learning as much as we can about how we show up, who we are and what we have to offer.

Going through the different stages of life with the different faces in front of us as we proceed, the last thing we are looking for is to be different. So, we are really up for a challenge in staying true to ourselves and loving who we are on the journey.
It's hard enough trying to fit in, let alone believing that we are the right fit at all, if we differ at all from all of those surrounding us. How hard it is to accept ourselves, when all the while our physical form and emotional stabilities are being tested.

Many of you, myself included; will say,
"You cannot pay me enough to go back to high school." I had an amazing experience.
But it certainly took a toll on me.
So why is this so . . .

If we look at why this is, what it is that makes us just cringe at the thought of bringing certain days back, this could be the very core of our path of finding our true connection with ourselves.

It is when we are at our most vulnerable that we must tap into the thoughts and feelings and see them as a tool for wondrous progression.
Instead of trying to find out who you are, while following the crowd, beg to differ!

"If I knew what I wanted, perhaps I would already have it instead of all these things I don't want."

Well, since you Put it That Way!

If you could have anything in the world, what would it be? Instead of thinking about why you don't have these things, or how you can possibly attain them, change it up a little bit!

Believe in the fact that you deserve what you want.
Openly communicate to the universe, clearly stating what you wish for, and watch for the
magic to take place.

We hear this many times, how people ask and they receive. What makes you any different than the rest?
We must believe sincerely that we are worthy of abundance. We must clearly define what we wish for.
Write it down. Put it in a letter to yourself.
Or, perhaps send yourself a card!

State all that you wish for as already having and mail it out to yourself as a gift to you . . .
Once you put it out there, the universe will accept it as such and do what it does best.

Give back.

Make your wishes real.

Don't just dream about them. Take steps to attain them. Put it out there and it will find its way to you.

"It seems whether I go in circles for an hour
or a day I end up right where I was!"

Cut to the Chase

It is true that no matter how you slice, dice or chop any situation, it is what it is. How we look at it and what we chose to do with it is what matters. We can walk away, hide, pull the sheets or the wool over our eyes—depending on how much you pay for your bedding—but one thing will always remain.

The same thing that was in front of us, before we attempted the escape, is still there. I speak from experience when I say it feels much worse dodging the issue, whether it be procrastinating a task, not picking up the phone to deal with pending bills, or bickering with a loved one. We are going to have to face the music at one point or another, so why not just stand tall and take it like a man? For all you women out there, we know we can be just as much a man as the best of them, so there is no discriminating here!

The recipe for a good life is so simple, so original, and doesn't need complicated tweaking or adding more ingredients to make it sweeter.

All we all want is to love, and to be loved.
But when we mask our lives with focusing on all the scary and unnecessary things, we take away from the original recipe.

Pay attention and pay up all that you have to, to take care and to be sure you are secure and safe in life. Don't run in circles in fear or in frustration. Just take the steps that are paving the way to success, one step at a time, moving forward.

We are so busy chasing our dreams and running from our nightmares that we can overlook the simple acts of kindness and the simple words and gestures to remind those that we love simply that we love them. We could be surprised at how subtle reminders that we are cared for can assist us in cutting all the red tape of fear and can help us take a step back and see what was hard for a moment is easier done with the support of our amazing circle of friends.

"The mind is a powerful thing.
Mine seems to go a hundred miles an hour;
That's power!"

Peace Out!

It really doesn't matter how many times we read it, tell it to ourselves, or intellectually just know that it is easier to get things done with a more relaxed mindset, sometimes it just doesn't seem to be the case.

Trying not to worry about the outcome of situations, but rather enjoying each moment for what it is and knowing that we will always be provided for, we can set ourselves up for more success rather than failure.

The more we focus on trying and trying to achieve something, we may be looking too closely at what we have not done yet to attain this goal.

Instead of fretting and fearful focus, sit back, relax and enjoy what you are doing. Since you are going to be doing it anyway, you may as well have fun.

Have faith!

Send peaceful energy to the universe and allow all of your stress to simply slide off of you.
Regain your composure and continue—calm, cool, collected, casual and, of course, confident that everything will be ok!

Peace Out!

"Our fears are only as big as we allow them to be.
I mean, how big is a cockroach, really? Yet, I will still
scream in terror at the sight."

Bugger Off!

If I didn't already know, a certain experience today led me to realize I not only create the abundance in my life, but also the fears and frights that come my way, especially the ones that linger for a while.

It seems it doesn't matter how connected you feel to life and love, you can still completely lose all composure in the presence of something as small as a cockroach along your passionate path. There will always be the few select and not so inviting pests, be it household, or held within your mind. It's how big and how much energy you give to them that is what makes or breaks you.

Things come to us when we are ready to accept and receive them. In this case, I had to mop my floor in excitement to feel ready to cleanse my surroundings and start my week with a vengeance. What I discovered was that I still have a few things to deal with and face that couldn't be ignored.

We may consciously think we are connected and coherent of our feelings, but there will lie underneath certain unconscious chaos that when we overlook it may take very tangible forms looking you straight in the eye, such as the cockroach (unfortunately for me, in my opinion, the least pleasurable of insects).

We may not be able to free ourselves from all the less than favorable things in life, but if we can, at least for ourselves and for those around us, acknowledge that which needs to be taken care of or that which we need to realize is much smaller than we lead on, perhaps the road will seem less difficult, and we can walk with confidence.
So what if a cockroach shares your path here or there? What has he really done "to you?" And, aren't we all connected?

Ok, maybe I am not ready to acknowledge everything just yet. The path of unconditional love is one very sensitive step at a time.

"Who is your sunshine, on a cloudy day?
Find them and make the most of it."

Yours, Truly

It is something to be blessed with acceptance from others. The fact of the matter is that not everyone is going to walk into our lives who accept us.
The more important aspect of this supposed unfortunate finding is that it is not unfortunate at all!
As we know, "like attracts like."

We are a mirror of who we come in contact with when we do come in contact. For many years when younger and perhaps more naïve and insecure, we attempted to follow the crowd whichever one was "in" at the time.

But once we grow as authentic individuals only then are we able to be the true "us" as we
will see it truly in others.

Those that do not accept you are showing you that you have attracted them because you do not accept something in yourself.

Once you acknowledge; thank, walk away and you start loving yourself—even just a glimpse and even in what may seem like a time of turmoil—you will meet just the right people for whom you will find such love as you are now finding love for yourself.

And, perhaps once you find that love in yourself, you can return to those who were once not so accepting, not only to now be accepted by them, but enabling them true acceptance of themselves through you.

That's what true friends are for—supportive sunshine on a cloudy day, genuinely and lovingly offering, without condition to walk through what you need to walk through and where, thus enabling you to see the true magic in yourself.

"We all fall in life.
But don't take it lying, or lying down."

Truth Be Told

Moms always know best. When we were younger, perhaps even now, if you are still so blessed to be in the presence of your Mom, she could always tell when we were being honest or far from it.

When we speak, whether or not being truthful, it all comes down to what we think and how we feel about ourselves.

What's more is that we all know how less than favorable it is to not be truthful to others. What holds true is we feel worse about ourselves in the long run.

We can lie to ourselves and we can lie to others. But truth be told, our minds can instantly shift to a confident state if we take a stand and start only speaking truth.

Just as pictures speak a thousand words, truth speaks volumes in creating a life of integrity, health and wellbeing.

And, if you are not sure if you are living a life of truth, just think of your Mom. If looks could kill, you will know you may have a bit more work to do.

"There are just some things in life that no matter how you slice it up, dress it up, or cover it up, you may simply just have to pass it up, to make room for the right fit for you."

If the Shoe Fits

Relationships are like shoe shopping... sometimes we will be so taken back by the style, color and even the brand, that we will work our hardest to squeeze our foot in the last pair that is a 1/2 size too small, going as far as to buy them still in hopes that with little stretch and wear here and there they will eventually fit.

It's the same in relationships. Even if the fit is not there, we will compromise our comfort where comfort should not be compromised.

Just as we will continue to look in the mirror, turning over and over, to see if the 1/2 size smaller even now complements our outfit, wasting precious hours staring, contemplating, forcing to believe it will be fine with a little fine tuning, we do the same in our own lives with others.

If the shoe fits, wear it. We all know how wonderful it feels to have that absolutely perfectly fitting shoe. We wouldn't give up the comfort and joy for the world, just like the right fit for us in love. We hold onto it near and dear to our hearts because our hearts glow in its presence! If the fit is too small or too big, or perhaps the wrong color; be nice to yourself and place it back for someone else to enjoy.

Chances are someone is doing the same for you.

"Sometimes it takes knowing very well what is not working in order to get things in working order in your life."

Works for Me!

We are often asked what it is that will make us happy and fulfill our lives. This can get us to stop and think—to re-evaluate our life's surroundings and put in perspective what true happiness is.

Before we are ready to understand that which makes us happy, we must look at why we may not be feeling this sense of fulfillment at this very moment.

What might we need to shift or change in order for the happiness to find its way through?
And more so, before we can look out for happiness, we must look in, and check in, on all that we are as it is right now.

We have such great friends and supporters in our lives that are so caring and willing to offer us so many opportunities and possibilities that may possibly lead us to the very happiness in which we search.

We must also remember-within us, whether or not we may feel lost and scared, lay the answers ready to come to us when we are ready to receive them.

So do what works at the time and walk through, continuing to follow your heart even if it seems to be walking toward darkness.

You can rest assured that the light is always waiting for you once you are ready for it. Do what works for you and never lose sight of your passions.

Never lose trust, love, and belief in always being taken care of, no matter how hard things may seem at the time.

You are always simply "where you are" in order to be ready to get to "where you are going." And only you know where that is.

"Take it for what it's worth, not for what you
expect to gain from it."

Just Like That!

Have you ever decided to do a little bit of tidying up,
to find yourself moving every piece of furniture,
opening and emptying every drawer and cupboard,
to find your entire living space in disarray?
You realize that what was once a small project to subtly enhance your
surroundings ends up in a giant mess.
You don't know how you will be able to put all the pieces together?

Many aspects of life have the same tone and story.
We overwhelm ourselves looking at the whole picture and all the pieces
we need to put together after we have made what we thought were
small changes for the good. We scare ourselves with uncertainty as to
where to begin to get back to whole.

If we can sit and breathe and take every piece of our lives that is in
disarray and focus solely on one small and delicate area at a time, most
of the puzzle will be pieced together before your eyes and you won't
even feel you have lifted a finger.

Don't get stuck on circumstance. This space you are in will change whether
it's the best place or the worst place you believe you have ever been.

Life is a series of lessons given one course at a time.
So, like a deliciously prepared 5 course meal, don't think of how
the appetizer tasted while you are eating the main course and don't
envision the sweetness of
the dessert when you are eating the salad.
Just enjoy every experience while you have it.
And don't worry if you flop on a dish now and then.
Practice will make perfect for you.

"It makes my whole day when someone takes a moment out of theirs for me."

Under the Circumstances

I woke up this morning and sat up to evaluate not only my surroundings
but my perception of it.
Considering where I am in my life vs. where I was last year at this time,
and 2 and then 3 years ago at this time,
I remember clearly my thoughts on 'me' and what I was accomplishing
and why then.

It is interesting to sit and ponder how things may end up looking going
forward or worse, worrying how everything will pan out.

But as I said to a friend, and maybe more for myself, no matter what we
think is going to happen, chances are something completely different
will come about anyhow.

So why not just focus on what is going on right now, and how we can
make this the best time,
no matter what we may have went through before or will later.

It doesn't matter how many times you go over it in your head what might
have been had you made a different decision, either years, weeks,
moments, or even days ago.
It simply cannot change the course of your life right now.

It is important to take ownership of this very moment, make choices that
will enable growth and prosperity, love and commitment to not only your
friends, and your loved ones,
but yourself and your capabilities.

Whatever the circumstances, you don't have to feel overwhelmed or
stuck in them or feel that they are hovering over you with a control that
is not yours to take hold of.
Under any circumstance you experience is a beautiful lesson to remind
you how much you have in you.

Just do the best to make choices that bring out the best in you and
you will see that every moment is just as precious as the next and just as
precious as you.

~ 47 ~

"We can be many things to many people; But who we are, to ourselves, is the mirror to our soul."

Above All Else

For many of us, our minds start running before we have had a chance to
take one step out of bed.
And to make matters more complicated, we play many roles depending
on the people we are
spending our time with.

As the day progresses, we interact with our friends, colleagues, and
families. Much of our energy can be exhausted, before we have even
had the opportunity to do for ourselves.

Many of us naturally feel the need to be there for all those that
surround us.
Yet we may not realize the toll it takes not only on our time, but on our
bodies as a whole.

We are aware that our moods are affected by our environment, not
only the place we are physically, but those who we include in this space.

In order to maintain balance, we must, above all else, be true to
ourselves and true to what it is that we need in our life that will maintain
harmony and true love.

Then, and only then, can you give enough without going above and
beyond what your body can handle, so you still have a handle on life.

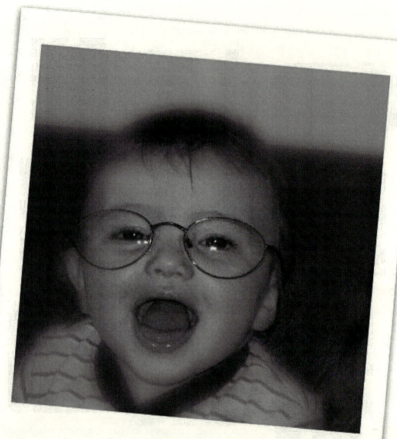

"No one can share our excitement or rain on our parade more than our own best friend—Oneself."

Beside Myself!

We've all heard the saying "I was just beside myself,"
when hearing of sheer excitement or overwhelming senses for a
situation having taken place.
We are so bombarded with exterior circumstances and events,
considering our social schedules, work atmospheres and
family functions.

We pretty much know what's going on in everyone's life around us, as
well in terms of the latest news and drama. Chances are we react with
quite a bit of empathetic passion
and understanding, having endured ourselves the many instances at
some point in our lives.

Although we can certainly use our connectivity and empathy to
support those in our lives for what they may be going through, we must
understand that lending an ear is far more effective than suggestions,
opinions and moreover hard hitting advice, simply because "we have
been there."

Every experience that one goes through, one goes through
as themselves, their particular past, their unique behaviors and
personalities, and, most importantly, their personal
relationships involved.

So be there for your friends because that is what friends are
for. However, realize that we must each make decisions, ponder
possibilities of how we, as individuals, need to evaluate our own
circumstances for growth on our own, in our own time.

I hope we are all so blessed to have our best friends surrounding us
when we need a hand to hold. However, remember you are your own
best friend. When you are beside yourself when something happens in
your life,
you are exactly where you need to be.

"Laugh until you cry. Smile until it hurts. Wish on falling stars; Let your friends catch you if you fall. But most of all live with your eyes wide open, opening your heart to all that you meet."

Top of the Morning to You!

There is really nothing better than the connection with a friend and sharing stories, experiences and, most of all, sharing fits of laughter.

Remember when you were younger and laughing so hard
you couldn't breathe?
Remember for some reason attempting to control your laughter but the word or thought that started it all would creep up causing you to laugh even harder?

There are so many things in life that may take us for a loop, so many responsibilities
that may flood our minds first thing in the morning and keep us from enjoying a great moment of just letting loose during the day.

While you must get those things done, do yourself a favor and just add a laugh to your
growing list of duties.

Maybe put this one at the top and the rest will be easier to get through.

"Running in life's marathon will be much easier when we stop getting ahead of ourselves!"

Not So Fast!

It's in my experience that it doesn't matter what shoes you buy, they cannot make you go any faster than your old worn out pair if you still have the string attaching both the right and left foot.

I noticed myself realizing this was so when trying a new pair on, looking for the mirror to see how good they looked on. They were still very much attached. Yet I was still trying to walk faster than I should knowingly.

But believe my look was not too classy, making my move so quickly with them still connected. It made me stop (I had to or I would have tripped over my own two feet) and think, "How do I run my life?"

I am always running.

We believe that we are to be busy to be productive! In my experience I have also gotten much more done when simply sitting still and letting my mind and body rest.

I have come up with the best strategies,
plans and creative ideas by lying down for five minutes.
It took doing the dishes, emptying the garbage and changing the paper towel roll while running to change the load of laundry to realize that not much comes to me when I am doing much too much!

If my mind is running a hundred miles an hour and going full force with a fistful of frenzying tasks, I cannot very well notice, let alone read the signs the universe is giving me to allow me to access my full potential.

So take it down a notch!

Take it from me!

"We have all the time in the world to worry, and not enough time to do what we need to do. You do the math . . ."

Wait a Minute

Have you ever opened your mouth just a little sooner than you wish
you had?
How many times have you "put your foot in your mouth" wishing you
had waited a minute, and perhaps pondered not only the conversation,
but your first reaction in defense to it?

We all have moments we wish we could take back;
sometimes they feel more like an eternity.

Needless to say, we have all said something we wish and know we could
have gone without saying.

And it goes without saying we would be in a very much more pleasant position
had we just left things better, unsaid.

Some things are meant to be spoken, and some things can be left without.
The best way to know which case scenario is the best case is to hold
off for a minute,
and think before we speak.

There may not seem to be enough time in the day to get all done that
we wish to get done; however, one thing is for sure;

In the precious moments we do have, we must make the most of them,
some of which used for silence, and listening to others,
without saying a word.

"They say be careful what you wish for.
I say be careful not to."

"Wishful Thinking"

I wish, I wish, I wish.
Remember growing up and looking up to the stars with
a wish so BIG you weren't sure you could even open your mouth, let
alone your mind to imagine
it could be possible?

But still, you saw that first star and better believe you were going to
make great use of it before you allowed your eyes to wander and see
yet another,
now knowing you couldn't very well.
"First star I see tonight, I wish I may I wish I might, have this wish I wish tonight."
And then you saw two!

Not only is it important to wish as much as we want,
we must wash out all the thoughts that are not allowing our minds to go
to the extremes,
setting our sights on our dreams.

When we creatively visualize our goals and our desires,
there are going to be roadblocks,
setbacks and mishaps that may stop us for a while,
delaying our travels to that very place we can only imagine being.

We are our own magicians, casting our wands, to manifest our wants.
Be a kid again, find that star and wish for what you wish to wish for! I
dare you not only to dream, but to wish for it to come true!
It's up to you to do!

Heck, wish not only on one but two!

"My brilliance shows up in my most
playful moments."

I Believe So

Things may seem to hit us from behind when we are not looking,
sideswipe us when our heads are in the clouds or give us whip lash when
we think we are focused and prepared for anything!

There is no right or wrong way to make adjustments.
If you are less than well adjusted in any area of your life, it is up to you
to do what you need to do and up to you what is best for you. But,
there is a great and exciting secret I can share with you that can allow
for preventive measures in regards to preparing for unforeseen hits that
may cause you to be a bit startled. Life is going to come at you from all
angles, be it the front, the side, or hit you from behind. It is what it is.

I can speak from experience when I say that if you look at things with
a positive mind, more often than not you will get positive back. Ever
notice how your day
just seems to follow suit, when you stub your foot while you were
positively and happily jumping out of bed ready to conquer the world?

Your whole mood shifts, your views on the day change and you quickly
change your mindset, causing your day to sometimes "seemingly" go
downhill from there.
If you can allow for each circumstance to not interfere with the next,
and take things in stride without breaking your positive stride, certainly
your day will only get better!
It is not childish to think everything is going to be just fine,
as the secret to happiness is paying attention to the wonders of the
world, not wondering why things less than satisfying are happening.

Take things as they come and walk it off to allow for the next moment to
go by without passing up every opportunity to be thankful for all that is
around you! And if you wish for things in your life to get better, believe
them to be so. Don't spend your time thinking you can't have it all.
Spend your time knowing you can!

"Listen carefully to your physical body's messages. For example, mine told me to take Monday off."

How Are You?

So much of our time is spent taking care of things that matter most to us.
This is the fact of life. What we care about most we take care of most.
And with taking care of others, we also pencil in taking care of business,
chores and other things that need care.
Sometimes, we can get exhausted trying to do
what never made us so exhausted doing before.

Why is it that one day, can you take on the world, and the other day,
you struggle just taking out the trash?
It all comes back to "you." How are you?

Our body, as we very well know, does not lie.

It doesn't know how to.
It strictly works on our behalf, and reacts to what is . . .
Like the heart only knows truth,
the body is just as loyal.

It speaks only what is—good, bad, happy, or sad.
It will speak how it feels. No made up stories or drama, just a simple
intuitive response as to how things are going while working away.

We must not only listen to our bodies,
we must love them as we would love another person.
We must care for our physical shells with all the love we can as it is the
only form we have on Earth to live,
laugh and love.

So, if your body has something to say, take a moment to listen,
so it doesn't have to yell!

"How much energy do you put on the struggles you are dealing with in your life, verses the great and wonderful things you have in your life?"

Point Taken

Tell me—how many times have you woken up,
and looked around, wondering "where am I?"
Then of course, you realize . . .

Ah yes, I am not only where I left myself before falling asleep, but I am
actually just where I expected myself to be, considering all my choices
to this point.

Creating chaos can be conquered by shifting our energy to the
positive and eradicating the negative.
We must look at what we need to work on.
But at what point is it unhealthy focusing on the scarcity in our lives?

And the answer to this can be making a point of acknowledging what
lies deep in our hearts that can very well and pretty well be the answer to
"our life's very question" of what will make us happy.

If we can make a point to take into consideration all that is most
important in our lives before we give energy and worry to all that we can
so very much do without, then perhaps the whole point to our story can
be summed up by first asking ourselves;
What's my point?

Secondly . . . Acting on it.

"So much from our past we carry with us,
latching on to us like magnets,
causing us to remain static in our lives."

Static Cling

Have you ever realized after a whole day of wearing your pants that there was a sock stuck to the inside?

We have all had experiences with static cling in one form or another. Sometimes it would feel next to impossible to remove the items!

We can take this situation and apply it to life, as well.

Not moving forward, not believing in our powers, and not allowing us the growth that not only will help us, but others in which we connect!

For one reason or another, we continually notice these mind tapes sticking with us, acting like they have our best interest at heart. Yet we know better, don't we?

What is clinging to you, causing a "Static" situation?

And what do you need to use to rid this and "bounce" out of the traditional stand still and move into the magic of life in abundance?

Don't let static cling hold you back from
being the best you ever!
Be static free and know you are worth it!

"The key to living not only a successful life, but a meaningful life, is to allow ourselves to experience each moment for what it has to offer."

One Moment, Please

Our minds love to wander, not to mention ponder so many things other than what is happening to us in our lives at this very moment.

Many times we will be in conversations with people without actually engaging fully, therefore not fully considerate in taking time out to be present.

Our relationships with those we love should take precedence over our thoughts, when communicating, and the only way to ensure this is to be present in the moment.

We have all the time in the world to think about time spent in the past, or what the future may hold for us.

Taking the time to just be with those who surround us and truly involve ourselves to our fullest in relating and enjoying time that is "now" is time well spent.
So don't spend each moment thinking of moments already gone or moments to come.
That is neither here nor there!

"There is nothing so warm and fuzzy like the support of those around us to keep us safe."

Mighty Oaks from Little Acorns Grow

How will it happen? When will it happen?
We are always so worried and wondering about the next steps in our
life that we sometimes overwhelm ourselves with just what steps to take
to get there.
So many times we can be confused and scared and perhaps a bit
frustrated wondering when we will reap the benefits for all of our hard work.

Many times, we feel almost as though perhaps we haven't been doing
enough, because if we get back tenfold what we put out there, we
shake our heads
because it hasn't come yet. What have we been doing wrong? There
is no way to measure just when we will see all great things come back
to us from everything we are and everything we do. One thing in life,
however, we can measure, it is how we measure up to the best us.
If we can walk and talk and breathe being the best us we can be, we
don't have to worry about whether or not our ship will come in. We will
just know that the journey we are on is that of upmost integrity.
Therefore, we can just be and be patient.
We are all going to slip up once in a while. But in doing so, perhaps we
can see the lesson in knowing that we will always be provided for, and
we will always be loved and cared for all we have to do is love and care.
It is so simple. An oak tree, the symbol of strength and endurance,
doesn't stand so tall in the forest simply because of its roots. Rather,
from the support of all that surrounds it to get it to its highest.
We are just the same.
We all desire to love and to be loved.
And in doing so, we all have the strength to grow to
become the greatest us we can be.
So do just that!

"The only difference between fiction and
non-fiction is which one I believe is true."

What's My Line?

I may not be a psychologist on paper, but as a writer, a woman, a sister,
a friend, an aunt, and a little girl (when I let myself be), what happens
in my life depends on me and what I chose to accept, reject, tolerate,
enable, or disregard as truth.

Life is a simple class in Psychology 101.
Everything we are, breathe, believe and act upon comes from our minds,
our thoughts, our fears and our trust in ourselves and in each other.

We all have different roles we play in our lives and the lives of others.
We have roles in the world as a whole.

To look at the economy, and it's positioning in current times, it begins
and ends with the mind.

The economy is not something separate from us. The economy is us.
But it seems as though we are all standing, waiting, biting our nails, like
actors, actresses, waiting for the paper, the media, the storyline to give
us our lines as to what to say next, and what to do and be next, and how
to show up.

We can act like we are puppets and characters in a play, or we can take
it upon ourselves to create for ourselves and each other an economy
that is rich in spirit, which will lead to more rich in security, not just
financially, but emotionally.

Whoever says that we are going through hard times took the first step.
It's he who follows through that takes the last.

What's my line?
As a writer, I will write it myself.

"We must always be prepared for when the opportunity of a lifetime knocks on our door. I keep mascara and lip gloss on me at all times."

You Are Cordially Invited . . .

There is nothing quite like getting an invitation in the mail for a high class gala, an event or a party of some sort that leaves you feeling a sense of unique style and success! How blessed you feel to be part of a "select" few people who are invited to mingle with the best of them, share and listen to stories of many accomplished and perhaps highly academic achievers! In life, we always hope and wish to be on the list with the best of them, don't we? We secretly hunger and crave for the prestigious status and all the goodies that come with it! Don't we?
While it is wonderful, and powerful to be involved with the best of the best, waiting and wishing for an invitation in the mail may be a pipe dream if you are not
taking actions to fulfill that dream!

We won't always be invited to the "A" list parties and we may not have the opportunity to schmooze with the highest rank successors in the world. But know this:
However you believe yourself the ability to achieve all that you want in your life is an
"Open Invitation."
You choose the date of this event or events, dress attire is also to your desire;
and you can choose the time and the place for all of this to unfold!

So many options in this thing called life!
The occasion and recognitions for all your successes are completely open and up to you to plan!

The only thing you need to ask yourself is . . .
"What WILL I WEAR?"

"Why is it, I ask, that we have so many things on our 'to do' lists that we simply do not want to do?"

Sticky Notes

We all keep a list of things that need to be done during the day. And as much as we are all the same in keeping notes, we are all just that much the same in not having the time to execute the tasks at hand.

Who in our lives tells us that half of the things
we have to do during that day, have to be on our list?
Of course, we are not so unique that we don't have to take out the trash whatever trash is to us; brush our teeth, take time out to make dinner, or grab take out. But, ultimately, we own our own lives.

So, we need to, if our list is not all so desirable, check in as to why we check off so many things on our list as done, not to mention even put on our list what we want to put off because it is not fulfilling
our personal passions.

Put on your list tasks that stick with you because you cannot wait to accomplish them! If we are going to follow a "to do" list, at least make it do something for us, because at the end of the day, we all have the same thoughts, we all want to be the best "us" we can be.

And, if we are wasting our time with wasteful tasks not to mention wasteful thoughts, we are certainly not attacking the tasks at hand to attain our triumphs!

So do it—create a "to do" list that sticks to creating your success!
And stick to it!

"Life is about taking what you have and rolling with it.
Perhaps you will roll with the punches. Perhaps
you will roll dice that you hadn't expected."

Please Do!

How many times have you wondered when you did something, what would have happened if you would have done something else in its place instead?

What about the times you have wondered if you did something instead of nothing at all? As long as you are doing something, you are far more advanced than those who think and do not do. You cannot be successful if you do not have a vision or a plan to gain success. And if by chance, your success is not at the place you wish so deeply you were, as long as you put your heart and soul in what you want, you will always get back what you put in.
Success does not happen overnight.

But tomorrow is always another day and no matter what you have done today, you are bound to have tomorrow. Put in today that of which you wish to have tomorrow and at least that of which you put in yesterday. But to roll with it, no matter what it is, is what makes it all the worthwhile. If you are wondering what if you did this or that, instead of the other?
Just do this, that or the other, and let all things fall into place, as they will, having done something, at least.

"I sometimes wonder what would happen
if I did one thing at a time."

Cruise Control

It's hard enough getting the momentum to start a project or task from the beginning, isn't it?
Now, we have all been there when we realize, after starting that the task at hand, that it really isn't as chaotic a chore after all.

It just took starting it. The rest was easy.

We have all been there, when after starting a project with all excitement and charisma,
we have been sidetracked by this thing called "life" resulting in setting aside the project for another priority.

What happens when we do this, the momentum it takes to reintroduce this project and go back is the same amount needed to start it again.

Instead of starting and stopping, allow yourself to live it in "cruise control." Enable life's happenings to happen as they will, and you can still carry on
without throwing things overboard when it all seems like too much.

Don't think of jumping ship when the going gets a bit tough. When the tides are high, you can always guarantee smooth sailing ahead!

"They say a dream deferred shrivels up like a raisin in the sun. Imagine? I certainly know my dreams are far too important to just shrivel up."

By The Way

If we are so adamant about making our dreams come true, we must then give others the opportunity to know just how it is we ensure the actions we take to fulfill our hearts desires are carried out.

We must write it down, step by step, a full documentation, a full understanding of how we have been so careful in implementing a plan to create
the dreams of our lives to become now our reality!

Create our plan of action, if you will.

You know to give to others to follow—to follow their dreams. Just like we so attentively follow our own!

This will enable others to create their own
steps to success!
With our help!

And, if perhaps we must go back, ourselves, in need a bit of a reminder as to how to go about it? It will be there ready for us to follow.

Just in case, I mean.
We know we already have it all planned.
It's all under control.

All your dreams can come true.
It's simply up to you.

"Once we realize we must not take each other's slips personally, we will be more than understanding in our relationships."

Slippery When Wet

We are not perfect.
We have all made choices that were not perhaps in our best interest.
We are beings, living and learning.

It comes down to understanding and forgiving ourselves and each
other, holding each other's hand when we need support, and
not judging
someone for their path.

We must make a commitment to be with our loved ones and offer support
while on their path, support of others as their life is lived, understanding
that we must allow each other the given right to slip and sometimes fall.

Relating is the readiness to pick each other up
when we are need of a pick-me-up.
No one does anything to us.
We simply accept or reject their miseries.
If we can see that other's miseries and others' pain is not about us, but
simply theirs, we can release the attachment we may have taken on,
and instead make sure our loved ones know that we love them.

We can see that this is their path to slip on.
And, we have our own, as well.

But to hold hands through the slip ups will lessen the fall. When things
come up and misery takes place again—and it will, because this is
life—being there and being the support system
that our loved ones need is all we can give.
And, it just feels great!

"If my mind is capable enough to dream
it up, the hardest part is done."

Dream On!

What is it going to take for us to believe that we are not only entitled to all that we desire, but that the capabilities to achieve this lies within. It's in the palm of our hands. We just have to open up to it.

I have been on the side of despair just as much as having been on the side of conquering some insurmountable feats in my life. We all have.

Each and every one of us has been through that which we may have temporarily deemed impossible.

As much as we can worry for the worst things to happen, we can use that same amount of energy to visualize and create in our minds what we dream to be in our lives.

With life's challenges come rewards of self worth, self reliance and self love. I can brave a storm as long as I know that I am the one who walked it for me for all the right reasons.

Do what you must for you and pay attention to all that your thoughts are telling you. Have only your best interest at heart.

We all pay the price for our actions. So if you want to make life easy, act on your dreams, walk with integrity, and wear the right shoes for the weather.

The results will be priceless!

"No one can make or break you but you.
The stage is yours, so break a leg!"

Off The Rack

May I start by clearly admitting that there is nothing I enjoy more than a great sale. As a woman, I thrive on clearance items, 50% off items, and yes, I will buy three in one color. Let' be honest—if it is a limited time offer,
I am going to be "smart" with my money!

But, when it comes to us, as individuals both male and female, why do we sell ourselves so short?

I am not the only one sitting back now to reflect. And I know before this sentence ends, you have counted at least 2-5 ways in which you have certainly sold yourself short.

It doesn't take a genius or an opinion poll to know that each and every one of us, deep down inside, knows of a passion or two that we wish to follow.

But once we recognize them, we place a price tag on ourselves as not worthy enough to buy into the thought of this "possible" soon to be priceless item of
intrigue in our minds.

Leave the bargains for the store.
Buy as many items as you need in as many colors as you think you need while the sale is on.

But please . . .
Take the tag off your mindset that brags a bargain.

And certainly don't spend so much time racking your brain as to why you can't do something amazing today, tomorrow, and for the rest of your life.

You can't place a price tag on passionate living.
It's free for the taking.

"No matter what the battle,
if we are still here; we got through it."

Motion Picture

Life as we know it is a sequence of experiences, and happenings, one second at a time.

While we go about performing our everyday duties, we are performing in our everyday lives,
as we see fit, and as we so desire—desirably.

Not one experience is the same. Not one moment can be compared to another. Every single step we take carries us to the next, and there is no going back.
We cannot simply rewind the tape if we feel we missed something, or need to add something in to more properly continue the path.

Many times, we will stop, and reflect; perhaps taking much notice as to how we have come to where we have come, understanding why certain things took place, when during those times, we may have otherwise wondered.

Life is beautiful, and it will continue to be so, as long as you can see the beauty in it. Every motion in our lives has a picture worth a thousand words—many times, leaving us speechless. Leaving us in awe, and wanting more!

Take a moment, and capture it's beauty. Believe in the magic behind every motion.
Allow love and life to move you—to places you may not have otherwise known existed.

What you surround yourself with and what you focus on in your life will be your life.
So don't just live it; love it!

Be sure to create all that you wish to for you, as this life is all yours to create!
As far as the eye can see, will be!

"Do it all over again? Sure, why not.
Just let me change my shoes."

The Tie That Binds

Going back in our minds, we may shake our heads with "what was I thinking?" thinking of a select few people, way back in the day that we either were friends with, dated, or hey, maybe even married!

We look back and wonder why we did what we did, or who we did what we did it, with.

It is an interesting fact that we have changed dramatically since then. But moreover, we have changed dramatically because of then.

All too often we will analyze, judge, or as far as condescend the situations or worse, the people that we have experienced life with. And even worse, we will blame them for where we are today, if where we are just so happens to be less favorable than our dream life we are still waiting for to be handed to us, or for some, mailed to us with a first-class stamp.

Every instance, every person and every experience we have is so important. Yet, the most important part is that we are all connected and what allows us to grow and learn is everyone we have ties with, and all of the bonds we have created—of course some broken. Nonetheless, they have been brought to us to build our lives and our hearts.

Love is blind, perhaps.
But it opens our eyes to too many things to not let it in.
Don't lose sight of love, and embrace the ties that bind you to those you love. And, never forget to remind them that you do love them.

"Last time I checked, I was still me.
I guess I have big shoes to fill"

We'll See

I pray for so many things, hoping I will see some sort of answer,
patience being top of them all. I never wanted to lose sight of what was
important, but I always wanted to see answers to my prayers as soon
as possible!

Remember our parents' answers to so many questions?
Different question—always the same answer.
"We'll see!"

So many times in our own lives, we chose not to allow for the best
conclusion through proactive determination and ambition, but instead
wait for other
than ourselves for who we are and where we end up.

How is that possible that we can put limits on all things possible?
By choosing "us" how others see us, rather than who we are?

Let's believe that we are capable of all things possible and can create
all of the experiences we believe we can see, visible, and moreover,
possible for ourselves.

If I had known that I can have everything I ever wanted, ever—well . . .
I have a bit of catching up to do.

"Too bad life couldn't be like a skill testing question: Fun times + 100 X (Laughter + Adventure) - Broken Hearts= . . ."

So Far, So Good!

Sure, if we had it our way, we would exchange all the experiences
not so attractive that we have endured and add in more carefree, and
venturesome situations
to take their place. It's not always easy to wake up feeling like
everything is going splendid and our lives are superb when, in fact, we
may be feeling a lack for things we wished we had in our lives, things we
wish we had done differently, or as much as not done at all.

Of course, we all have days when it seems like to even set foot on the
floor may feel like it is setting a milestone, when our thoughts may be
miles from attending to any affirmative action.

But look at it this way; if you can look back on who you have been,
what you have done and who you have helped along the way, you may
notice that all the not so splendid experiences you have encountered
were integral for you to be strong enough and moreover courageous
enough to make the next decisions.

For as far as I can remember all of what I have personally experienced
was so fundamental to where I am now. Taking anything out of the
equation could perhaps be a recipe for disaster!

I think we should recognize that we have done a pretty good job so
far with our choices, including the few detours we may have taken, and
crossroads we have stopped and pondered on for a little longer than
we may think could have been.

So let's scrap any negative thoughts we may have otherwise accepted
and exchange them
for a good time!

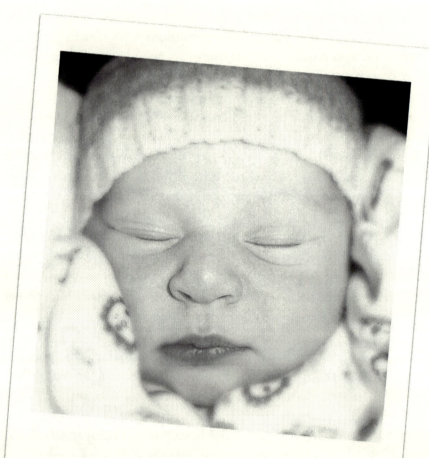

"If only we could put our inner clocks on vibrate."

Alarm Will Sound

Like clockwork... well, actually, literally clockwork...
our alarms will ring bright and early for us to start our day. Our days
start off with the trusty alarm.

As much as we not only detest this sound, many times in our attempts
to deny it, we will press snooze as much as we can without risking being
late getting to the pressing issues at work waiting for us.

Just as our alarms will sound in our homes, our inner alarms do just the
same to allow us to acknowledge when it is time to pay attention
to something.

Our inner alarms act like a warning sign when the subtle signs of our
intuition are not strong enough to grab our attention.

It's kind of like a strong cup of espresso to get our brains functioning
where it certainly wouldn't otherwise have the slightest clue.

These alarms sound loudly enough for us to have to stop and take
action. Whether or not we chose to listen and execute a task of growth
or press the emotional snooze button a few more times, we can be sure
that, just like clockwork,
the alarm will sound again.

We all have wake up calls. It's whether or not we chose to sleep through
them that make all the difference.

"They say you can't bring it with you.
But has anyone really ever tried?"

Handle with Care

When we were kids, we would at times be in awe of our parents' ability
to seemingly have a handle on things put in front of them.

Being grown ups, we sometimes wonder how they did it!

We sometimes wonder how we are going to do it.

Life's ups and downs are as inevitable as the weather.
No matter what the temperature, no matter how clear or gloomy the sky,
it will change and we will change with it.

Our lives are precious and so are our decisions to
handle circumstances surrounding what we attract in our lives.

How we do so is a reflection of how important we are to ourselves.

Just as careful as we are to label our most precious belongings as they
move on their journey with us in our lives, we must be just as adamant
about our choices
and how we handle our emotions and care for ourselves through our
own inner journeys.

So be sure to label your thoughts, choices,
emotions and decisions as carefully as you
would your belongings.

"FRAGILE: Handle with Care"

"No matter how it is delivered,
the truth still comes out just the same."

Who Am I Kidding?

With all of the relationship connections we have in our lifetime, not to mention, all at one time, let alone our relationship we are trying to work on with ourselves, it's no wonder we can get a bit confused about our feelings, our intentions and, of course, the intentions of those around us. When it all comes down to it, we truly in our hearts can sense a comfort, a trust and an acknowledgement of what relationships are working for us and what relationships we needn't try so hard on making work. Every last one of us speaks and breathes from our hearts, all the truth for any questions we need answered lives here. We can save a lot of turmoil and confusion by simply living from this space.

There are times when we must take the high road, in relationships, not trying to pave out a road, where a road needn't be paved. We cannot walk people's paths for them, or kid ourselves into believing so. Our hearts will tell us when things are out of alignment, and a shift is to take place.
We can, at this time, listen and move forward, or continue where we are—but this will only last for so long.
Who are we kidding?

Not all relationships are meant to work out to the very end of time. However, many are here for the time being and needed for us to not only figure out what we do want to surround ourselves with, but also what doesn't fit in our lives, to better our lives. And that is ok, too.

We owe it to ourselves to understand as much about ourselves so we can give to others in ways that will allow them to grow and be the best they can be, however that relationship may look like. We must understand that we shouldn't kid ourselves into believing that every connection is a lifetime of matrimony.

That's what friends are for, however they come and go, or come and stay. We can't have it all with everyone, or we would leave no one for everyone else. Although to have it all would be wonderful, wouldn't it?
Who am I kidding?

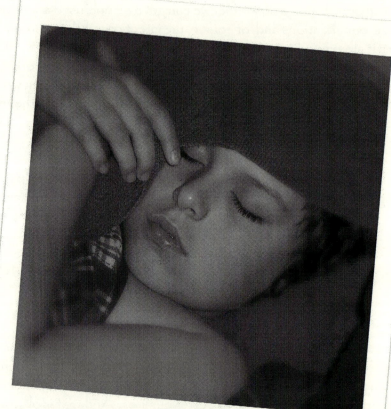

"Success doesn't happen overnight.
But a good night's sleep won't hurt
my chances of it happening!"

It Goes Without Saying

Putting something in place to invest for tomorrow as we live in the
present moment may not be the easiest
and simplest way to spend our energy.

We want to make the most of our moments,
but also want to be sure that we are considering the safety of our future.

There are so many stresses we all face individually that may make us
feel a bit alone, scared and often times a bit nervous as to what is the
next best thing to do.

But besides having our own personal fears,
we must realize it is in our own best interest to share our thoughts, open
to those who love us, and communicate what is on our minds.

You would be surprised as to how many friends
and people in your life are actually going through many of the same
issues and fears in their personal lives.

Sometimes by speaking our mind, we can acknowledge the best path
for us to take and make it
more clearly defined!

It goes without saying that friends lending an ear can be just the
support we need, but to go without saying anything we will never know!

"Some things all happen at once.
For all these things, all we need is each other."

One Fell Swoop

Maybe it is just me, but it seems that at a time
when we are reaching a higher level of spirituality and "awakening,"
as many of us may call it, we are also facing much despair and fear,
economically and socially.

Why is this so?

If we look deeper at all that is taking place,
we can see the protection of the universe
and its plan to ensure care among all and among all things
that are existing around us.

When it seems much is caving in,
either in our own lives or the world as a whole,
we are that much more intuitively preparing ourselves collectively to assist
and nurture under such duress.

Making a habit of working together and loving
and supporting each other makes getting through even
the toughest of times seemingly easier.

Not every day is going to be spent tip-toeing through the tulips.
However, if we can surround ourselves with those that help us grow
and help those who may need a bit more of a nudge to keep going,
we may be surprised at just how fast our weeds will die,
leaving room for the most beautiful flowers we ever saw.

It only takes one thought to change the world
and if we can do it in one fell swoop,
there is hope for us yet!

"I'd fail Chemistry. As an Entrepreneur,
I am too busy creating my own."

Fuel to the Fire

It goes without saying that the keys to success are patience and persistence. To be sure we are not expecting a quick fix, an "over night" miracle, but mostly to maintain something that is working and not losing sight and losing it before it's too late.

Whether it is business or personal, the same rule rings true.

As well as patience and persistence, it is also imperative that we nurture our relationships with a constant and positive process so we don't threaten neglecting the most important things that work to keep things going.

If we are expecting to get back something that we are not putting in, we will be wasting a lot of energy. We must continue to add fuel to our fire.

Like a flame in a fire, if we fail to keep it burning, the flames go out and it takes much more energy to rekindle.

If we can be more proactive in understanding what our relationships need and how to strengthen them, to keep them burning bright constantly, then we take out the guess work of constantly wondering why things are not working in the first place.

We all have paradigms that perhaps leave us feeling limited, or hindered beliefs of what our lives should look like, and what we should be doing, and how, and with who, based on the stigma of everything around us. We grew up being told what the norm is.

I say toss anything inhibiting your growth and add fuel to your fire.

"It's not so much the act of dreaming,
but more our willingness to act on them!"

If You Will

Waking up each morning, we are given a very generous opportunity.
Just as when we were younger during art class—given a blank paper,
crayons, markers, and paint. It was ours alone to do with it what we will.

We can look at our lives as the same fortuity of limitless creation.
As we chose one brush stroke one color at a time, perhaps mixing two
colors we didn't realize can manifest into something beyond our mind's
understanding. It is then that our world will open up to
boundless possibilities.

And just as perhaps when we were younger, our picture would not
serve us and we may crumble it up, throw it on the floor and start over,
we must be just as willing to do the same now.

Will you take the chance at starting over every day as a new day?

We have the opportunity to look back on what we have lived through,
how we chose to paint our picture, and what we have achieved. If we
feel we want to continue sketching, painting, or coloring from the same
canvas, let's do so. If we need to walk away from one that we don't know
what stroke next to take and work on a new piece rather than mark up a
potentially pretty piece then do it.

Be willing to follow your heart and be willing to paint the scenery of
your life, how you view it now. Only you know what colors work best
and what strokes
lead to success for you.

Draw out all that you feel inside and to master your own piece,
one movement at a time.
You may be surprised with the end result.

"They say variety is the spice of life.
I say a little Kahlua in my coffee
works just as good."

Check, Please!

So many things that we do, we do on autopilot.
We wake up to our alarms (press snooze about an average of 3 to 5 times), get up out of bed, brush our teeth, get breakfast, coffee and head off to work.
All too often, we may find ourselves a bit off when everything in our lives is seemingly on cue.

The more aware we are about our emotions, the easier it is to get through every day with ease and comfort.

We need to check in with where we are so we are not caught off guard by out of the blue breakdowns.

We are so good at what we do because we do it so often, that it is second nature for us. But as the days and the months go on, we wonder where the time has gone simply because we don't actually live in the present moment. We certainly make the most of our time by getting as much done in as little time as possible. However, when is it a good time to take time out for ourselves?

Our days will get hectic and the demands of life, family and social commitments may take up so much our time that we fail to commit to giving ourselves time to check in with our thoughts, and see how we, ourselves, are doing.

So while you are working, shopping, cooking, and giving to all those you love, in your life; make sure to treat yourself first.

"If advice is free for the taking,
can I still get a rain check?"

Raise the Bar

We all have so much in store, though sometimes we wonder what we are waiting for in life, that we can bypass the signs and messages that stand right in front of us telling us how far we have come. Energies will come in and remind us that we are in fact growing, and ok to grow.

There are going to be days when we may feel afraid to ask for a helping hand or to allow things into our lives that are supposedly "more" than we may feel we deserve.

If they are in front of us, being offered freely, we must at least give it that much, that it is free for the taking. People are here for each other to assist in raising the bar in life and holding their hands for us when we may feel this
bar is out of reach.

We tend to undervalue our presence in other's "now."
Just as we are being helped on our path, and being guided to where we need to go, we are just as much being the strength
for others who may not have the strength on their own
to continue on their path to greatness.
It just works that way.

We may have a broken dream here and there and may fear going forward because of so many fears that perhaps hinder our belief that we are capable of love, care and support.

But believe when I say that you can always find strength in every moment you have lived thus far. And what do you do if someone offers a helping hand to get
you to the next moment?

Just smile and say thank you.
It will prompt you to do just the same for someone else.

Would you want to take that amazing feeling from someone?
I didn't think so.

"Let's face life with showing love,
because let's face it, the show will go on . . ."

Front and Center

Who doesn't like a little drama?
Ok, admittedly, some of us enjoy it more than others,
but it's safe to say that in life we all have varying roles,
some are seemingly more dramatic at times.
Other times, we play more of a supporting role or perhaps just a by-stander.

No matter what role we play as the days go on, we can inevitably play
it as best we can. No one day leaves you more or less important than
the day before. So why act like it? There are going to be days we wish
we could hide under the covers, where there are other days we are so
excited to hop out of bed and get the day started, we may even forget
to wear underwear because we are so pumped. (Note: not a big deal, if
you can at least remember to put on your pants).

But, it is important that you wear the pants in your relationship with
yourself, and at least put in the attempt to show up 100% no matter
what the case may be.

In case you are ever wondering why you may still be waiting for that
Award Winning Life of glitz and glamour—whatever that is for you—
take a good hard look at how you play your part. Be sure to stand
front and center, allowing yourself to not only have the lights shine on
you, but to shine bright
with your unique talent.

You don't have to break a leg.
Just break out of your shell a little and prepare to accept a standing
ovation.
Own it.

Just don't push others off the stage in your
quest for success.
That's just bad form!

"I live a conscious life. I am very conscious of when it is time to close my mouth. I am half way there."

Let Sleeping Dogs Lie

It doesn't seem to matter how far we come, in terms of learning, once in a while our programs or egos can get the best of us.

Just because we are growing on our paths, whether spiritually or emotionally, our emotions are very powerful and can take the wheel—driving us sometimes out of our minds.

Thinking back to personal or professional conflicts in your life, maybe for some of us, not so far back; perhaps seem to endure much longer than anticipated. Can you sense a common theme?

It seems as though when we react based on our emotions, we can definitely stir the pot much more than if we are to take a look at the situation, perhaps stepping out of it emotionally, to look at what it is from a different standpoint.

All of us have been hurt in our lives at one point or another. It is not always an easy task to separate from our emotions when we are struggling with a conflict. Not only do we attack based on the emotions we are feeling at the moment, but our ego takes the initiative to remind us of all the other wonderful times we felt this way. This can cause chaos in our hearts and on the surface.

We can say hurtful things, and we can battle until we're blue in the face, when dealing with feelings based on our core emotions.

Just as emotions strike a physical response in our bodies, we may tend to physically strike out with partners, friends and family.

It only takes a small change in our awareness to shift our behaviors. So, next time you sense your emotions are about to get the best of you? Try your best to understand where they are coming from and why.

And perhaps when you do so, you can leave them in the past and let sleeping dogs lie.

"The cost of living is high enough. I don't want to pay the price of living someone else's life."

Musical Chairs

Think of an experience you have lived through, whether a tough
time, traumatic or worry some. What may come to mind is the support
surrounding
the experience while you endured it, rather than just the experience
itself. Or perhaps it's the music that you played to get you through.

Sometimes, the hardest times can come when you feel
the pressure of having to react or be a certain way in a certain instance,
depending on how you feel regarding expectations from your friends and family.
This causes a sense of doubt, guilt and fear
for making the wrong choices.

Every episode is individual, since each of us can only bring into it
the knowledge, the understanding and our own personalities and
behaviors. We cannot sit in on someone else's experience.

Just as many have expectations or hopes for us,
we also will find ourselves perhaps whispering under our breaths for
others to make decisions, or root for them to "make the right choices"
we feel are right.
Fortunately, there is no right or wrong,
as what can be right for one would be wrong for another. It just simply
depends on the person.

Our most important role for each other is to be sure that we give the
energy of support while each of us walks our path, perhaps tripping a few
times over each other. Worse, we may be falling over our own two feet.

You owe it to yourself to do what you feel is best
at the best of times and at the worst of times. What's the worst that
can happen if you give it your all? Having a friend there to listen to you
when you may not even be able to hear yourself think, can be music to
your ears.

"I would rather give thanks than give up!"

Once Upon A Time

"...And they lived happily ever after."
Wouldn't that be amazing, if all the stories and fables we were told as
children were true, not just tales?
But they are just that, right? Tales... Fables...

The tests and turmoil of the princes and princesses, and the lessons
and experiences brought on by evil goblins and enemies unlike anything
we have accompanied. Thank goodness for fiction.
I don't know about you, but if I found a dragon in my forest, I may not
find life so enchanting.

However, I have learned of strength attained after
all the mental and physical anguish cast
upon the characters.

In the end, whether all turned out well or whether pain
was indeed endured but evil indeed eradicated, the moral of the story
would leave us spellbound with a deep understanding of life and its
lessons.

Everything we experience in our own lives is just as told in a tale. It's
true.

We live, we love and once in a while, we hurt and we move on, bigger,
better and stronger. We carry with us all the armor that we feel will
personally protect us and,
hopefully, we can let our guard down once in a while to participate and
progress. We don't have to be a prince or princess to play a big part in
the story.

As for happily ever after; I believe in fairy tales.

Why is it one day I feel on top of the world, other days I feel caught between two worlds and some days I wonder what in the world is going on?"

Members Only

As we get older, not only do our bodies change, but our interests, our talents, our creative outlets and, therefore, our networks.

We were always taught as we grew up about the power of sharing and of getting involved with groups and clubs to assist us in our social development.

We would try out for our favorite sports teams, educational programs, or sign up to be involved in a multitude of events that may not only peak our interest, but hone in on where our strengths lie.

If you are like most of us, we feel a need to be part of something, to help us in identifying ourselves and our personalities.

Even as we grow older and stronger, there will be days where we just feel like we don't fit in anywhere specific causing us an identity crisis or perhaps as much as a breakdown.

We all owe it to ourselves to breakdown our barriers and stimulate our lives with a motivation and focus that will serve as a positive outlet and a balance from the hectic work lives we are leading.

If we can take time for ourselves and lead ourselves in the right direction by writing down and looking closely at what we enjoy doing and where we enjoying going, perhaps we won't get stuck doing something or being somewhere we just don't want to do or be.

And, we are not always going to be part of every crowd.
So take those times to be on your own and make the most of every minute! There will always be times where we are pulled in every direction.

Don't get stuck in a rut!

"If someone gave me not just a penny for my thoughts, but another penny for every second thought, I would be one rich woman!"

Inquire Within

All of us have select friends that we call as soon as certain "things" hit the fan or when push comes to shove, and then again when the dust settles, to thank them for enduring us throughout the storm.

It is so wonderful to have unconditional support that allows us comfort through tough times and to remind us, even when we are acting crazy, that we are not crazy. Well, most of the time, anyway.

It is important to have friends to confide in and a hand to reach out to hold when we may feel as though we cannot take hold of situations or sometimes what life has thrown us. However, we must believe that all that we need comes from within.

Our thoughts can get the best of us and our hearts can find us confused many times throughout our lives.

Having second thoughts about what we want, where we are and how we are feeling is absolutely normal. We all have times where we fear that making one decision may be so detrimental we start over analyzing our every step, sometimes to the point of stepping down from making any decision at all.

Be ok with stopping and sitting with yourself before moving forward if you are not sure which move to make.

Not making a decision is a decision in itself.
Make time for yourself and believe that
you already know.

When opportunity arises,
Inquire Within

"We cannot very well be inspired and be
encouraged by others and not inspire
and encourage others ourselves!"

Enough Already

When speaking of spiritual growth, we often approach
the subject of who we surround ourselves with.
Who are the five people we spend most of our time with? We are the
sum of these people.

Not only is it who we spend our time with,
but it is also important to take inventory who we are in this equation.

For as much as we are influenced by our surroundings,
we are just as influential, in turn.

When looking at what we have to bring to the table,
we must also allow ourselves the possibilities that what we have is
enough. While we always have room for improvement, having the mental
state that what we have is great already, will allow us the capability and,
moreover, the confidence to see others
through in times of need.

We needn't worry if what we have to offer is good enough. Instead,
give all that we are capable of giving.
And when we allow ourselves time for ourselves,
work on bettering the great that we already are!

So, if you are wondering if you are good enough—enough already!

"I know it was worth it if I have the scars to prove it."

Make Your Mark

When the new day sets in, we set up in our minds
what we see ourselves tackling and accomplishing.
Many times, as much as we would like, a new day does not mean a clean
slate to start over. For most of us, we will carry forward unfinished
business from the day
before that may make us feel a bit overwhelmed
to get going.

As with business, our personal lives can take a toll from all the
unfinished issues and energy that we still, today carry with us from
yesterday's situations
that we have not officially closed out.

But this doesn't have to be a deal stopper for moving on. Instead it can
be a realization of what is holding us back. What we have not dealt with
yet could be set in place.

Just as it is best when finishing a day of work to organize and take
inventory on what has been left over and needs to be taken care of, we
must also take care
of ourselves on a personal level if we are making changes and moving
forward to a new chapter, just as we would a new day.

Take the lessons and the marks that may have even as much as scarred
you, but caused you a deeper understanding of who you are, of course.
Just be sure to close out any unfinished personal business and take
personal responsibility when you need so you can move on with a clear
head and a clean slate.

Only then will you be ready to make your mark on your own.

"Change is never easy.
But it is easier when you lighten up."

Baggage Claim

In our lives we go through many transitions, whether personal,
professional, spiritual . . .
you get the picture.

As the picture of our lives changes,
we not only seem to change our exterior environment,
but our inner selves and all that we carry with us in our minds and in our hearts.

Our decisions as to what we keep with us, is far more important than
we might think. Much of this may be far more beneficial to leave behind
rather than to weigh us down as we progress.

When we decide to move on or to make a shift in our personal course,
we must consider, of course, what we need and needn't pack with us.
We all have "baggage" which can hinder our path, if we chose to bring
it with us, instead of learn from it, and leave it well enough alone as we
walk forward.

As we gather all of the necessities to take on a trip, we always realize
we could have done without many of the items that are not really going
to serve us in our journey. We can do just the same in our travels in
personal growth.

Claim all that you own, emotionally,
so you can work through your life with knowing how you got to here, but
know that going forward you are not obligated to continue with everything!

So lighten up!

"True vision is not seen with the eyes.
It is felt in the heart."

By The Book

When was the last time you felt successful?
Can you even remember?
To look further, we must understand in our minds what our "vision of success" is. How it looks to us.

Our ideas of success will differ not only geographically and demographically, but they will certainly differ dependent upon what we have been breed to believe success was growing up in our own households and in what we surrounded ourselves with, starting with our thoughts.

To live in a society where success is measured by money, education, assets, or specific accomplishments recognized by highly acclaimed decision makers, we may individually be ultimately brushing off our own true sense of success.

To truly be successful is to truly be following our dreams, taking individual steps to be in integrity with our set vision, and ourselves. To walk a path that we, for ourselves, are creating with our best interest at heart and those around us.

We don't have to attempt to be what others have been or do what others are doing to make it successfully, in our lives.

Measure your success by doing what feels right in your heart, creating your own destiny based on using your own skills and talents and actively working on continually being the best "you."

Don't feel pressured to go by the book on success, unless you wrote the book yourself.

"It's not where you stand in life,
but how you stand in life."

Out on a Limb

Since our early childhood,
we have experienced many situations—many interesting or complex affairs—
that have ultimately lead us to where we stand today and how we stand
up and show up in our
lives and our relationships.

Our personalities, our behaviors and our views on a multitude of issues
and instances will highly differ no matter how close and similar we may
be to our friends
and those with whom we share our lives.

While some of us will be more open to taking a risk and putting it all out
there with vulnerabilities visible, it sometimes will take others a bit of
time before they can trust in taking an extra step out of their comfort
zone to see what the world has to offer.

Both of which are understandable once we understand a person in
their authenticity.

We are all growing at our appropriate pace.

Just as one may feel it best to take the risk right away,
and jump into life from the get go, we must sometimes go out on a limb,
in our own mindset, and allow for others around us to walk their path as
their own, comfortably, without pushing them to show up where they are
not ready to show up.

Showing up in relationships is showing support for each other no
matter where we stand. Just be sure not to compromise your own place
and posture.

"It is one thing to know what our best qualities
are, but another thing to use them."

Please Stand Clear

In our lifetime we not only spend much of our time learning, but we are
then asked to evaluate which subjects we thrive in and therefore will
'major' in during our days of educational lessons, tests and finals.
Not so finally, we attempt to find the roles we can jump into that will
utilize our talents and challenge us in a positive and impactful way while
we hope to make a deep impact on others.

While it is great to do a great job, we are all entitled to do that which
makes us happy and fulfilled, not only successfully, but wholeheartedly.
There are millions of opportunities out there, but it is important to take
on that which that brings out the best version of us rather than trying
to fill shoes that are not ours.

When push comes to shove there is nothing wrong
with doing all we can to conquer the circumstances to get ahead. Just don't
push yourself to be or do something that is not called upon you to do.
If you are uncertain as to where you see yourself and what you need in
your life, take a moment to evaluate your strengths, your interests and
your capabilities!

When making life decisions, whether big or small,
make a point to stand clear in your intentions
and watch nature take its course.

"Sometimes the simplest thing to do
can seem the hardest."

None the Less

Whether we are thinking in our sleep,
while we eat or while we are supposed
to be using our thoughts to focus on our jobs,
we are always constantly thinking.
If we look at animals in action, they are not thinking of the past, or the
future, but what is in front of them, taken for what it is, now.

It is our thoughts that create our lives, since we manifest that of which
we create in our minds. We know this, and yet we still consciously, as
much as subconsciously, make decisions to think of and worry about
less important things which are not allowing us to engage
in a life that is abundant.

We surround ourselves with only what we feel worthy of.
We create and attempt to maintain relationships that may not be in our best
interest simply because we think we must make it work, or we have failed.

Failure doesn't come from acting on something,
even if it means leaving a situation, a job or an environment that is not
serving you. By taking positive action, we are using our strength to
create a life that
will allow us to flourish.

By doing so, we are not just serving ourselves,
but we are also enabling those around us to grow in a better and
healthier direction.

It is important not only to focus on the great things that we can have.
It is imperative that we take a step toward dissipating the thoughts
and the areas in our life that we are focusing on, that are giving us less
rather than more.

So, while you are building and manifesting the life of your dreams, be
easy on yourself. Take your thoughts and . . .
. . . None the Less.

"Perhaps the secret to the truth
is to believe in our own."

BYOB

As a child, I was brought up Catholic.
I attended church every Sunday with my parents.
As I grew older, my views on life and everything that surrounded me
began to expand as I expanded my horizons and set out to find my true
passions and with that, my own truth.

Along my journey, I was fortunate not only to meet and build amazing
friendships and relationships—some that last to this day and others
that have since gone
—but also to understand so many different beliefs that people have
and have grown up practicing that have given them the opportunity to
feel faithful
and hopeful for life, and all it has to offer.

If we had to believe everything that everyone we have met believes, we
would barely have enough
time to breathe.

Believe me, there was a time when I thought I should understand every
religion in order to understand everyone in my life.

That is not the case. We can all try to state our case and try to
push our beliefs on others. But as it has it, the only thing we need to
understand and practice is love, kindness, and integrity, first within.

To accept someone for their beliefs and embrace that they are truly
on their own path to truth is what our world just may need in order to
open up to a compassionate and accepting energy.

So, if you are ever invited to a party and don't know what to bring?
Bring your own belief. And leave any judgment on others at the door.

"Sometimes we must go in the entirely opposite direction to make any real progress."

Enter at Your Own Risk

Our minds are very powerful things. We know this.
We read about it, we talk about it and most importantly, we experience
it for ourselves, just how profoundly preeminent our emotions are in our
lives and how our minds set the stage for all that
we live and breathe.

Our connection between our emotional well being
and our physical well being are so directly correlated
and we can become aware of how possibly exhausted our minds are
when our bodies decide
to tire out as well.

As with our inner alarms, our physical selves speak up loudly for us to
hear and take into account that there is need of a resting period.

Many of us have experienced burnout by not allowing our bodies to rest.
We see the signs that it is time to slow down, but we keep going anyway.

This may not only be a sign that our bodies need some TLC, but it
could also be looked on as a possible sign that what we need to see in
our lives—direction wise—may only be understood when we slow down
the pace
and perhaps stop for a moment to take in what we may not otherwise
have been able to take in if we are taking off at a hundred miles an hour
in every direction.

So, if your body sneaks in a sniffle and a sneeze,
surrender to a sweet sleep and follow your dreams.

"Knowing where to begin is half the battle."

Divide and Conquer

Not only is there so much unknown in our lives,
there are so many things we feel we need to understand completely and
thoroughly before we can begin a project, task or job.

Because we may be so intimidated by so many things that are in our
face at once, we tend to throw our hands up in the air, fearing with
frustration and admitting defeat before we even set
our feet in to test the waters.

If we can take all that we need to achieve, create a plan of action that
involves divvying up the priorities so we can see clearly what we have
in front of us along the way of success, perhaps we can take all the
despair we are carrying with us and finally conquer the chaos and in
turn the circumstance we fear the most.

Don't lose your way because you feel you are not strong enough to
take on battles! Banish any belief that is not supporting you and bring
on all the achievements you can handle!

We can all have a handle on life, one cupful of confidence at a time.

"My idea of a good time is to make it one!"

Phone a Friend

We have all been there. Times get tough.
We feel in a rut and things just aren't going as we planned for them to.

Sometimes even standing on our own two feet seems like an impossible feat.

No matter what challenge, what issue or what traumatic situation you
are faced with, many times just the voice,
shoulder or hand of a friend can make even
the hardest of times seem bearable.

We are all going to go through many tests of strength in our lives, be it
financial hurdles, personal paranoia, you name it. But if you can name
off a few amazing and supportive friends that will take your call and be
there for you when you are in need of them, things will look up. I can
promise you that.

I know. I have been there and I have had the financial hurdles from long
distance dialogues to prove it!

Not to say that we can cure a chaos or crisis with just a call, but there is
definitely hope for us yet when we can call out to those who love us and
are willing to listen to us when we may feel like we are on our last breath.

Just breathe in and breathe easy knowing not only will this, too, pass,
but remember also not to pass up
the opportunity to phone a friend when you need.
They are always literally a phone call away.

"Whatever you do, add a little music to it."

Surround Sound

Buses, car horns, police sirens, children screaming, dogs barking . . . I use my mornings to walk in the world and look at it in all it has to offer. No iPod or no MP3 player during this time, to mask out all the noise. Instead take in the surroundings with no judgment, no expectation, but just what is.

Surrendering to the surrounding sounds of life is an amazing step in living in the moment, just for what it has to offer, not for what you expect from it.

As it is imperative to see through life through every lovely and perhaps not so light and gay offering, it is in the acceptance of what surrounds us that allows us a wonderful way of looking into what we are involved in.

We have every opportunity in front of us to be where we want to be. Perhaps not overnight, but certainly with due time. Surrounding ourselves with positivity, love, and courageous, supportive friends is instrumental in our growth and the growth of others. But first, we must accept what is going on around us and acknowledge the world in its order.

Take a step in the world with eyes of truth and acceptance, making a point of taking a moment to breathe in the realness of it all.

Live in the moment and make the best of it as best you can for what it is worth. There is music all around us. Sometimes it is just about turning up your awareness a notch to make out the words.

"Buy me things and I will thank you.
Bake me things and I will love you forever."

No Purchase Necessary

Do you ever notice that when you feel something is missing, the first instinct we do as humans is reach for the credit card and the keys and make a mad dash to purchase in our attempts to fill whatever the void is we are experiencing?

I know for me, in my many years as a woman, I can recall the many times when I felt empty and my first course of action was to fill my place, emptying my wallet.

We cannot release the emotional burdens we carry by burdening ourselves, financially, and we certainly will not be in a better place simply because our place is looking a bit better from the new and temporarily exciting purchases.

In our attempts to find that happiness that we are all seemingly in pursuit of, no new purse or suit will have the answers, no matter how much time we spend and money we spend trying to mask ourselves with things.

The thing is this: we have everything inside of us that we need. So forget this need to surround ourselves with things that have no value in our lives, no matter what the price tag says.

There is value in believing that we are priceless and worth everything our heart desires to attain with no purchase necessary!

"It is not the have,
but the hold, that is dear."

Hold on for Dear Life

We have all lost things or people in our lives,
and in reflection, have wondered if we had done or said something
different would things be different. It is never easy, going through a
transition, when we may have only wished for things to be different.

So much of our time is wasted with thinking and focusing on the things
in our lives which, if taken away, would actually not mean much and
would mean no real loss.

So, why is it that we hold on to those things?

If you take inventory in your life as to what you hold dear, be sure, while
you still have it near and dear to your heart that you cherish and care
for it with all of your heart.

Jobs, material belongings,
even memories will come and go.
Don't let go of what is important,
of what you cannot imagine living without.

"Even if I wanted to do it all over again,
I wouldn't know where to begin.
So, I will just keep on going."

Come Again?

It seems that every time I second guess myself,
something or someone so amazing will come into my view to remind me
not to waste time guessing about life and simply spend it living.

We are all so often staring so far into the future and over our
shoulders, hoping it will work out, but not so much as to realize that we
create our future now.
And, our past no longer exists.

We are actually very smart and more "on it" than we give ourselves
credit for. And, when situations arise that we feel we already took care
of, just know that there is yet another lesson in it. It is not that you
failed the first time, but that you took care of what you could, with what
you knew how, and with all that you had in you at the time.

There are absolutely no wrong turns in life.

If you do a u-turn and come again to where you already were, don't
wonder why. Whether you think you are repeating something,
you are not.

We are all progressing and ever changing, moment to moment, different
and better than we
were moments before.

Even when life throws us for a loop and we feel we have went back a
few steps, we can just step back, look up and enjoy the view. It won't
ever come again.

"Much of life's confusion can be conquered
by the simple act of smiling.
At least you will look less confused."

However

Our minds are bombarded with programs, judgment,
fear and past experiences. It is not always so easy to be certain
what is right in front of us. No matter how many books we have read
through, or self development courses we have worked through, we are
complicated beings, ever changing, every single day.

How can we know everything?

We can, however, embrace what is in front of us at any given moment,
whether we completely understand it or not. We must instead
understand how it can help us see
who we are and how we are seeing the world.
Every moment has something very powerful.
It's a matter of how you look at it.

Not to mention that we struggle trying to always figure out how we are
going to get from point A to point B, when all the while as long as we
know why we want something,
the "how" will soon follow, not only effortlessly,
but understandably.

We can have all we want. The universe is generous like that. So don't
spend so much time wondering the "how in the world you are going to
get there", or "how the heck did this or that happen to you", so much
that you forget why you wanted something to begin with. You will lose
your mind completely!

We can be patient and gentle with ourselves, making a point, from point
A to point B, to be as open as we can, as loving and respectful as we
can and as true to ourselves,
as we can, however we can. We know it's not the destination so much as the
journey. Believe that however your life is right now is just how it is to be.
However, you have the power to make it better,
if you wish.

Just don't ask me how!

"We all have wings.
We just haven't used them yet."

"Light as a Feather"

Walking yesterday, a beautiful black feather breezed along my foot just close enough for me to catch it before it was to continue its effortless journey throughout the universe.

I use many of my daily experiences to my advantage when it comes to seeing things in my own life for what they are. Isn't that the point?

We can walk with our eyes closed and come up with confusion for what is going on so we don't have to feel it was our creation, or we can allow the moments to take our breath away. In some cases make us stop dead in our tracks, to catch our breath and grasp what is going on. In my case, I was to grasp a feather and realize what this meant for me and for my life at that very moment.

Our trials are only as easy or as hard as we allow them. We can breeze through things and focus on the solutions, or we can be weighed down by them, not being able to see that there is a light of day.

All of us will get heavily hit once in a while, every last one of us.

Understanding that we are capable of changing not only our circumstances, but our views on them, we can then create all that we ever imagined and be accepting when not everything falls on our laps like we would all like.

We have all heard it: "This, too, shall pass." But you can take it one step further and be open to all the magical messages that pass you along the way, that are yours for the taking. Perhaps you will then be able to breathe easier when scarier than normal circumstances may leave you trying to catch your breath.

"I may feel small, sometimes.
But I secretly know I can move the world
with a simple thought. To me, that's huge."

Strong as an Ox

Interestingly enough, sometimes we may think we get it,
but there is still much more that we need to learn.
A feather over my feet obviously didn't allow me the perspective of
how things can be easy if we allow them to.
I have since met the bird. Without coincidence, I walked to a place
out from my usual path in my own backyard, to find a bird, not just a
feather, fall at my feet. She was beautiful and gentle, yet I did have to
ask why she remained so close, not scared so much as to fly from me
as we stood toe to toe. She was wounded at the chest, not allowing
her to fly. I wept in shock. She looked still gentle, and so put together,
though she was far from whole. She stood breathing, as I started to
lose composure wondering what to do to help as she remained without
any sign of fright. Hours had passed as she stood there, still breathing,
believing in life as it may. Not knowing for certain that hers would be a
life possibly taken today. I prayed and I thought of her as the sun would
go down, As luck would have it, high winds and soon rain.
In the desert, I wondered of what fright she must feel,
all alone, and still bearing her pain.
But she stood there, alone, took all that came her way.
She put all of her doubts aside.
This small wounded healer. So innocent and sweet,
not once has she ever since cried.
With the fear of her passing, finding her not surviving her storm, at last I
walked away and then slept.
I awoke to a backyard minus one wounded,
for she was furthest from anything inept.
She had not only experienced, she sat patiently and persistently,
believed that life takes its course.
And, if you can open your heart out to faith and to love,
there is no need for a space of remorse.
A small bird has taught the largest of lessons of which I will carry each
day. That it is not that which happens,
but how you react and your strength when come as it may.

"I am at liberty to say what I feel and
be who I am. What more is there?"

Statue of Liberty

We may struggle, we may second guess and many times we may doubt.
We may blame, we may fall victim to situations and circumstances that
come our way, not knowing why we go through what we go through or
how we will get through.

For all of us at one point or another in our lives,
we had been certain there was no way around the hurt,
the pain or the trauma that we were experiencing.

Then the next day came; and the day after.
Slowly, we were able heal. Slowly, we were able to raise our heads and
be ready for the beauty that would continue to manifest in front of us.

We were ready to let go of the hardship, not always to forget, as
many times we must keep in our hearts a piece of our pain, but to move
forward, with a deeper understanding, not only of our lives,
but of our purpose.

It doesn't matter what country you are from.
The universal laws of life are just that, universal.

We are all connected in one way or another, no matter what land we
landed on.

To stand tall and represent our world as one, whether we are working
moms, husbands, leaders, givers, laborers, encouragers or healers, we
all have the liberty to represent ourselves as who we are.

And, make the world an even better place
because of it.

Be the Statue of Liberty. You have it in you.
Bring out the best in you.

"Today can be measured not only by how many breaths
we take, but how many friends get us through when
perhaps we have forgotten to breathe altogether."

Under the Influence

It's true that no matter what, we must get ourselves through to the end
of the day.
But when we have an amazing support system to remind us that we are
worth everything our heart desires, the day doesn't look so dreary.

When we are just about to throw in the towel on a project or on a goal
that seems so far out of reach, there is something to be said for the
phone ringing or an email popping into your inbox with words
that leave you speechless from support.

Our circle of friends says a lot about us, from what our leisure hobbies
consist of, perhaps the music we listen to, or personality traits we carry.
We are who we hang out with, right?

To be supported, cared for and nurtured by friends that want to see
us succeed,
so much that they will go the extra mile to push us to the finish line,
means so much.

Words cannot capture the gratitude and appreciation we have for
our friends and their influence to allow us to reach the highest of our
potentials and then some...

... and then some.

"I'll bet if I started each day with a big bowl
of ice cream, I couldn't help but smile
every minute thereafter."

Opening Statement

It is interesting how I have learned that so much of our day is simply a continuation of thoughts manifested from the very early moments.

Right when we open our eyes and take our first breath in the morning, we have planned each and every moment thereafter.

How do you start your day?

What are your opening statements to yourself?
Do you exude positive excitement?
Do you exclude pessimistic resistance?

Though situations that come up will change our thoughts and reactions as we proceed, how we initially react to things will be triggered from our subconscious tapes dependent on how we felt bright and early.

By waking up and creating a positive energy, whether it be meditation, walking, reading, eating a healthy breakfast, or personal mantras to manifest magic in our days, we can make the day be however we see fit.

It is important to remember that if things don't go according to plan, they certainly can get better. If we can take a moment and make it the best from the beginning, imagine the possibilities!

Do you have any arguments?

"You cannot see clearly all the amazing signs
in front of you if you are occupying your vision
staring in the rear view mirror."

Right Turn Only

What is a typical day like for you?
If we reflect after a day's worth of hard work,
commuting, communications; whether personal or professional, meal breaks,
coffee breaks, perhaps "mental & physical breakdowns" due to all of
the above, we may see a pattern that is worth taking a closer look at.

Though all that we must get accomplished in a day is not only taxing,
tedious and many times tiring, our views on it are what makes it so.

Most of what flies around our minds, while we are flying around our
houses and our hometowns trying to achieve as much as we can is that
we second guess if we are spending our time wisely. We always have in
our minds a question of whether or not we are doing the right thing.
What should we being doing instead?

Rather than attacking ourselves not only for struggling with the
tasks at hand, but struggling with whether or not the other handful
of household and other duties should be attacked instead, we must,
without a fight, accept what we are doing. We can trust that our lives
are being lived just as it should be.

We have enough going on in the day. The last thing we need to do is
spend the extra time we have wondering
if we lived our day the right way.

There is only one way to go and it's always the right way.

So when you come to a crossroads and you don't know which way to go.
Remember to simply follow the signs.

"Right Turn Only"

"What we think we then believe.
Whether true or untrue, and we then live out."

How Thoughtful!

We love it when others surprise us with a kind gesture,
and act of appreciation, or an offering of some sort
to be shown how much we are cared for.

As it is nice to receive such great things, it is just as wonderful a feeling
to give! When we are thoughtful and take the time to express our
gratitude, it brings up our energy and allows us to feel more alive and
positive naturally.

Just as healthy as it is to give out and receive,
we must take note of what we are feeding our minds and thus receiving
and living out as a result.

We are very aware that we live and breathe through our thoughts.

Think about it!

Whatever you chose to think may be limiting you from what may be
right in front of your very eyes!

How many times have you over reacted about something before
communicating to someone involved, creating a whole story in your head,
only to find out all was absolutely absurd?

In order to live a life of abundance, love, compassion and genuine care,
we must take care and be mindful of each and everything we think about.

There is a book in all of us. It's crucial while creating our wonderful
autobiography, that we are not writing too much fiction and drama, as
the story of our lives are the stories of our minds.

What do you want your story to be about?

"Be not what you think you are, but
what you know you can become."

I'll be the Judge of That

It's no surprise that we walk around wondering,
worried what other people are thinking of us.
We have, since before we can remember, felt this pressure to conform
to specific beliefs,
to go "with the crowd" or feel as though we must act in a way that will
generally be accepted as normal.
There are, as well, many of us who like to go against the grain and who,
perhaps, have set the stage above these so called beliefs in which the
others soon follow.

Once we start to lead a more "aware" life and begin a shift in
transforming into recognizing that we are not simply here to enjoy the
material aspects of which our lives exist in, but rather, to enjoy life and
the energy that it entails as intangible,
we may fear this sense of no longer belonging.

Are we now learning to accept ourselves, to find true love for ourselves,
whereas before we looked to others for acceptance and approval?

Aren't we now at a higher playing field now that we are living
on a higher plane? Wouldn't this mean a more calm and serene
understanding of life and what we can enjoy from it, rather than what we
can get from others?

Absolutely!

By making a change in our lives, though so immensely positive; we have
again the pressure of being "out of the norm" to many with whom we
communicate. No one said change it easy. But to take the step toward
personal growth and understanding of what great opportunities will
come out of living the best "us" we can be, we must make the decision
of what is best for us, even if it seems to fail to meet the consensus of
those around us.

For me, I'll be the judge of that!

"From the very start of our lives, we come into the world like none other. The world is for us to see through our eyes and our eyes only."

Bona Fide

We can stand beside someone either in the playground, on the basketball court, on the construction site or in the board room, and no matter what we are looking at, be it the same thing someone else may be looking it, we will always see things differently from those playing, standing or working beside us.

We share this world with millions of beautiful creatures. We have the opportunity to share beautiful and meaningful experiences with many of these millions, if we are lucky enough. The connecting of souls happens like magic. We are on this earth to offer insight, care, love, and whatever it may be to others because of what we, ourselves, stand for.

When ego gets in the way of our authenticity, many things can happen. We look for love and acceptance through the expectations of others and as a result lose our selves in the process. Friends, family members and media shape our views of life right from the get go, making it a difficult task to maintain and embrace our individual selves. But without living authentically, we will not be able to truly experience all that we were put on this earth to experience.

To make matters more complicated, by following our ego's guide to be accepted as anything other than "us", we are also taking from all those around us whose souls are here to connect with ours. We can feel our energies not in alignment with the universe when we feel we are stumbling through life, perhaps even stubbing our toes, walking into walls and feeling an actual physical sense of being off kilter, living through our ego. Not feeling like we are getting from life what we truly would like to attract, we will lack a sense of accomplishment and lack a sense that we are in true alignment.

Be all that you can be so you can ensure that you are making not just the most of your life while in this world, but helping those so blessed with the opportunity to be touched by you, all of what your authentic self stands for. And remember, you can lean on others once in a while, too.

"Gold may get you a lot of things, but it won't mean a thing, if you cannot share it with loved ones."

Shuck It

Remember the old saying "The World is My Oyster?"
What did this mean?

Many would believe it meant as diverse as one with money having all the
opportunity, to the world being openly available to any who took the
opportunity to be open to it!

We all know a select one or two people who repeatedly seem to strike all the
luck! But as luck would have it, we all have the power to surround ourselves
with all the riches we can ever imagine!

However, what is "rich" to you?
This is the key to unlocking the barriers or to "shucking" the oyster of
which the jewel you rightly deserve resides.

And even more so, it is imperative to understand that though we must
be open to the receiving of assistance and recognition of those who
help us on our path, guiding us as we break down our beliefs holding us
back, we must be willing to shuck our own oyster.

It is a feeling of euphoria once we have reached the riches beyond our
wildest dreams, the riches that lie within our being, the owner of our
path to riches.
So, know that "the world is your oyster" and . . .

SHUCK IT!

"Believe that you can get through,
because all you have to do is decide to!"

Oh My!

Day in and day out, we are exposed to many situations, encounters and sometimes mishaps that make us stand back and cause us to decompose our existing confident composures.

This can leave us remaining confused as to who, what, when, where and why certain predicaments take place.

While we are aware that we are fully responsible for how we walk this road of life, we will certainly find days where issues, clearly out of our control, will come up!

And as they do, and will continue to, we must do all we can in our personal power to accept all for what it is.
We must embrace our own strength that will get us by during these seemingly somewhat
"struggle filled" situations.

While we don't have to own the exterior issue, we must own our response to it. This is the secret to success!

So, if any crazy catastrophe causes your response of Oh My! Take in and observe this as an opportunity to test your strength to the fullest!

"What we have in our lives now, and working with it, will get us to where we want to be."

Carry On Now

Looking back at what we have been through in our lives,
what we carry with us, and most importantly how we wish to carry on,
consider and reflect upon one thing and one thing only.

Many hours can be used up wishing and wanting, hoping and dreaming.
And there is nothing wrong with a
strong vision.

But if we spend our time getting all worked up in our heads with the
scarcity and the "don't haves", we waste the energy and time that we can
be enjoying and utilizing all that we "do have" to help us along our way!

Make use of your days, moment to moment.
Carry yourself with confidence for all that you carry with you on
this journey.

Realize that you have carried yourself up to this point and all that you
carry with you will allow you to keep going, and be just fine still.

Make use of your resources. You would be surprised at just what
amazing things can come out of seemingly small opportunities. It is most
important to see things not only for what they are and how they can
help you, but also to see things in a different light.
Let's get creative!

Everything you carry with you along your path is everything you need.
Don't doubt where you are. Don't stress if at times you feel stuck in a
corner. There will always be room for more happiness, more growth and
more abundance.
So just relax...
Whatever it is you have, appreciate it and Carry On...Now!

"There is no dream too daring to draw out; no passion so preposterous that we should hold it in."

And Action!

How many of us have dreams that we wish to ignite into reality? How many of us do not believe ourselves worthy enough to go forward, to take an energy from deep within our hearts that will enable us the power to bring about into our life, into our waking days, what we may only believe is alive in the dark hours of our sleeping subconscious?

We all have dreams. We all have aspirations.
Some of us share two or a few with others we are close to. Some of our dreams are so diverse, so unique, that we may perhaps lock them into our programs as too outrageous to share.

We need more of us. We need all of us to grab a hold of life! Let's all fill it with as many of our dreams as we can physically fill life with. And just when we
think we are fulfilled?

Let's fill life with yet one more fulfilled dream still!

"What a relief to know I can let things go."

Press Release

Take a moment for yourself.
What things, people and circumstances do you not
even think twice to add to your life's pile, not even realizing that you
have a choice in the matter, to add only to this pile all that will help you
on your path to the best you?

When we start our day, when we wake to new breath, new heartbeats
ever so blessed to be given, we must not only savor the moments given
to us, but cherish the choice to pick and chose what comes and goes in
our lives. Both to keep with us what will allow growth, and to let go what
hinders our successes and that is ok.

Much of what we keep we may be doing so as programmed belief that
we are obligated to hold on to such things, when, in truth, we should see
the obligation in the release of such things that deter us from being the
most amazing us we can ever
imagine being.

We are the writers of the "press release" of our lives and what we wish
to include in our stories we must take ownership for.

And at any time, we are also entitled to edit, make additions and also
delete any statements that no longer hold true for us.

Only when we are able and willing to press "release" on these buttons
that are being pressed by us, inhibiting our growth, are we able to open
our hearts to the beauty—first and foremost within   and now radiating
out into the world to show others from our experience, with love, what it
means to pursue the real you.

"The world is made up of amazing talent that each one carries within us. But we first must go beyond our belief that it is beyond us to bear."

It's Beyond Me!

When we were kids, it was so embedded in our minds what success was to look like. If we think back as to what we envisioned our lives to be when we were younger, it usually, more often than not, was very typical. At least I know it was for me.

Go to school, hopefully reach post-secondary education, graduate, marry, have children, have more children, perhaps have a dual income raising family, save for retirement and then retire.

Not to say that this is not a wonderfully planned life of sheer pleasure and fulfillment. But it is hard to go against the grain and think outside of this typical structure and see success in a different light. Even if we have already achieved this and it is what we strived for, there is always a chance we may want to take a look at the dreams and aspirations still inside our hearts to come out.

Believing that we can make our way another way can be hard to comprehend, when we have many heads turn if we make a turn that is other than the straight and narrow.
This may deter us from seeing our true passion and believing that our talents and creativity can actually be our path to success, not just a day dream on our 3 o'clock coffee break.

No one can tell you where your dreams are going to take you.
You have all the power in the world to manifest them into reality as long as you can think them up in your head.

What are your dreams? Are they beyond you to express and materialize? If you have already answered the first question, do yourself a favor and answer 'no' to the second.

Let your doubt be beyond you.
It's beyond me!

"If we had to be serious all of the time,
we would burn out even more than we
already do."

Spare Me

Throughout our days, much of our spare time is filled with gossip the latest trends in technology, fashion and many other miscellaneous and mundane fill-ins to take us to a more casual level of being where we don't have to think so much.

We look to these various forms of banter to escape from the more serious demeanor we portray while fulfilling our obligations at work and at home to find a sense of balance.

Although we are worthy of taking a break from all the responsibility and duties that take up most of our Monday to Friday schedules, there is much more out there to balance out our hectic hours.

It is integral for us to spend our spare time filled with activities and pursuits that will bring us more long term fulfillment, rather than instant gratification.

If you take inventory of your spare time and how it is actually spent and whether or not is actually in line with your long term goals, you may wish to make small changes to revamp your schedule.

Just like we may plan our long term financial freedom, it is just as important to spend our free time wisely. What we surround ourselves with now will directly influence what happens years from now. It's never too early to invest in our future.

"It's hard to stop and smell the roses, when you don't take a moment to step foot outside."

Get Out!

It is our belief, more often than not, that we need to be working hard, stressed, and under the gun, to feel that we are accomplishing something, and to make it worthwhile for the paycheck at the end of the week.

Taking on challenges is great for the mind and great for the soul. This allows us to see ourselves for the productive and effective individuals that we are.

Of course, no one is going to pay the bills for us, and no one will mow the lawn, take out the trash and feed the kids, that is, if we are fortunate enough to be blessed with little ones. Yet as well as it is imperative to make sure we are making ends meet, we must put at the forefront of our minds, making sure our needs are met!

Be sure to watch out and take care of all that is around you, to have balance in your days and your surroundings.
Be sure to watch for what is going on within, or you may find yourself a little off-centre.

One of the best ways to get a grip on grueling days of taking care of all the chaos is to get out and enjoy a breath of fresh air once in a while!

The chaos will be there when you return.
But if you return with a clear head and a clear mind,
you may be that much more able to tackle the trivia that
surrounds today!

So, if you hear someone struggling with an issue,
a stressful situation or simply in need of a shift?

Take my suggestion!
"Get Out!"

"Life can be a bed of roses, if we just think of the thorns as reminders that we are strong enough to take life in, whatever the experience!"

La Vie En Rose

"When you change the way you look at things,
things change."
Author Unknown

It is true, isn't it?
We can look at things in ways, that either allow us to grow or allow us
to falter.
It doesn't matter what the issue, what the circumstance. For every
single situation,
it has been looked at by someone, in both a positive way and another in
a negative way.

Things are going to come up in our lives and
we may want to sit and say "why me?"
Either way, they will come up!
We cannot control all that happens,
but we can control our choices in reaction to it.

To be able to walk our path and be open to embracing
every experience
as an opportunity to grow and learn, we can walk a little taller!

To be at peace with life, for all it has to offer, and really allow it and say
"I see this for what it is, and I chose to react to this in the best way that
will allow me
to be in integrity, in love and in peace with myself as I go through this,"
we can rest assured with faith that just as everything we have
experienced,
to now, has happened and has passed into our past, this, too, shall pass.

"No matter what the relationship, the end result is only as strong as the foundation in which it started."

Cornerstone

In order to build a strong foundation, there are many tools needed and many materials,
as well that are crucial for ensuring the strongest building possible.

We need these tools to build a structure that can withstand the strongest of winds,
the harshest of elements, and still come out intact.

We know that there will be days when the sun will not always shine its brightest,
putting a damper on emotional confidences we may otherwise have.

However, like we prepare for the winter storms, the tornados, and the surprising hits of hail, lightning and rain, we can take a stand with building inner and outer "bonds."

Many circumstances will hit home, so be sure your home is secure and you have your cornerstones in place before you start building.

And never rush construction. Each step of the process is just as important as the last.

Start off on the right foot.

"One cannot breed war in an environment created out of love. With love, there is no room for negative."

Love, Actually

What if I told you that I have the answer that is going to transform the world? Create harmony in the most chaotic of circumstances? Clear up all confusion over right or wrong, prejudice, fear, hate, turmoil, hostility and, most importantly, the breed of war amongst countries, families, friends and the worst war of all, the war with ourselves?

There are many statistics in life that we never really pay attention to, that do not directly influence us in our personal lives, to be of any matter to us.

I am not a scientific individual, nor am I a "numbers" person as much as I would love to be.

What I do know, is that what matter most in our lives is matters of the heart.

What I do know is that the odds are in our favor, "hands down" when we choose love over any other feeling optioned to us, as then, nothing can stand in our way.

The world is in no way disconnected from itself in any form, so, even if you feel too small to make a change, you are statistically mistaken!

We know that it only takes one person to make a difference.

That is why we have world leaders, many who have as one person changed the world, made a world of difference in the way the world thinks, the ways it runs and the way it reacts.

You don't have to change the world to make a world of difference. Just start by choosing love in all that you do and the rest will take care of itself. We are not as small as we think we are. We are just as powerful as the most powerful people we know.

What's love got to do with it?

EVERYTHING!

"If the day comes that I know it all,
I am throwing in the towel."

Don't Mind If I Don't

Imagine if you had all the answers in advance?
You started out on this beautiful course called life and someone at the
"starting line" handed you a sheet with all the answers, all of the turns
to take, all of the people to meet who will only be the perfect people to
meet, and they have all the answers for you for
your journey.

Imagine you were told your heart will never be torn. You will never
have to turn in circles to find the right track. You will always just know
for sure all that you need and want as it will be labeled just that and
everything will always just be as you could have ever imagined?

Midnight streets will have you swept off your feet to the light of day
and life would always be just so sweet.

Unfortunately, not everything in life will last. We will not always have
the answers to life's questions.

We will not always be sure that what we are doing is right.
We will have to get thrown once in a while. And, we will realize that life
does go on, we will be swept off our feet, once in a while, in love.
And, for all the times we get carried to the next step, we will, as well, be
able to carry someone to
their next step, too.

Mistakes will be made, fears will take over. The seemingly easy road
will sometimes end up being the hardest. Many of the times the path
that we are most afraid to take Will be the path to greatness.

Inevitably, this path you may not know is the best path for you. But if
you follow your heart, which only knows love, then chances are you can
rest assured that you are making the right choices.

If you are not sure and you shiver along this path, you can ask your
heart to remind you that you will be ok.
It knows that you don't have all the answers. And, it loves to carry you.
So don't mind if you don't!

In Closing . . .

Dust Yourself Off

Dust yourself off every time that you fall.
Chances are this was not the worst fall of them all.

Don't count the bruises. Mistakes are your friend.
There is magic in the lesson, you'll learn in the end.

Even if you chose the shoes you always love to wear;
You can still fall, still stumble, whether seemingly fair or unfair.

Live in the moment. Don't fear for the trip.
Don't worry if you end up in pants with a rip.

It's worth it to walk, even skip, if you will.
As falling down can happen, even if you stand still!

So crawl, run, hike, tread; do one or do all!
Just dust yourself off every time that you fall!

LoVe,

LuCy sMiLeS

Lucy Smiles

'This is why I write.'
L.S.

Your smiles, I find them so thought provoking and inspirational
as I go through such change these days.
All the best!
Alyce

I just wanted to say thank you!! I just love your thoughtful creations!
As with many other days your little words inspired me.
Thank you! Always, Anita

Wow! That's amazing! I am going through a period where I keep asking myself
"Am I good enough for what I want to deliver to others" and your answer is
perfect: "Enough already!"—What an amazing synchronicity!! C x

Wow you have so much potential that one day soon you are going to
take off and fly higher than you ever thought possible. It's a new day
and another chance at life! Love, James

Hi Diane, I wanted to tell you that usually your messages are exactly
where I am that day. Last two messages have been bang on.
Thank you for putting my feelings on the paper for me.
I appreciate your writing, Love Kam

You are fabulous with these encouraging notes! Thanks, you are a
true form of inspiration.

I love your writing because you speak from your heart. You have the
heart of a poet.
You are truly blessed for you are capable of such intense and deep
feelings. This book,
this work comes from so deep within you, it's you. You couldn't not
write it! Love Paul

Hi Lucy—you're so clever and creative too! Blessings to you . . . I love
this "Press Release" smile and want your permission to include it in my
classes PLEASE!!!! Since I teach about "LIVING CHOICES"
this is another way of saying it and I love it—Thanks a million . . . . Raywyn

Get Published, Inc!
Thorofare, NJ 08086
11 September 2009
BA2009254